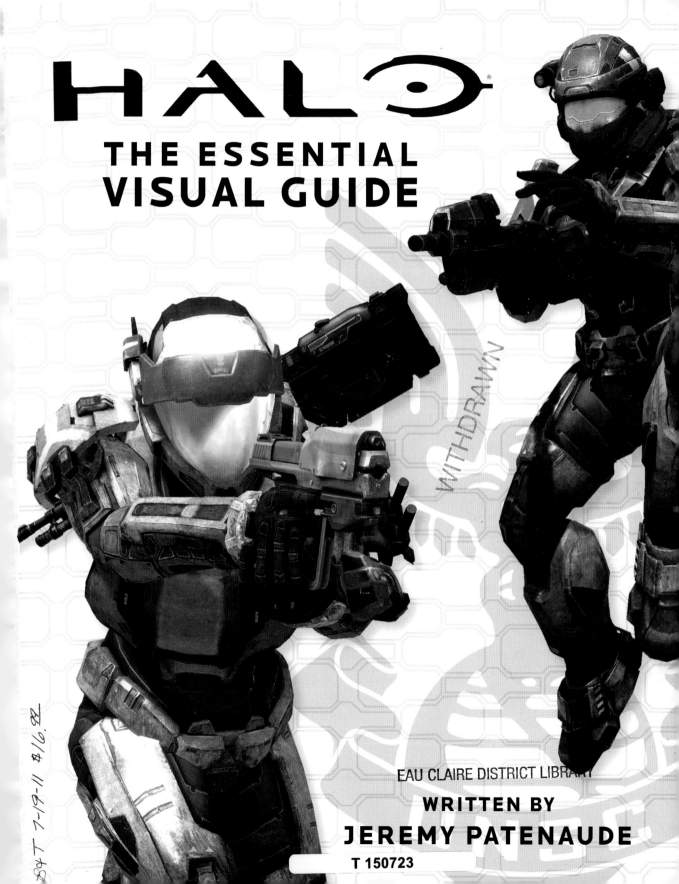

HALO®
THE ESSENTIAL VISUAL GUIDE

WRITTEN BY
JEREMY PATENAUDE

CONTENTS

THE HALO UNIVERSE is packed with brave heroes, deadly enemies, intriguing species, high-tech weapons, vehicles, and ships.

Halo The Essential Visual Guide explores over 200 entries and reveals insights into their roles in the battle for humanity's survival.

Entries are color-coded by affiliation and arranged in alphabetical order according to their most common names, for example "Keyes, Jacob," "Mickey," and "Lord Hood." All entries are listed opposite for easy reference.

 UNSC

COVENANT

FORERUNNERS

 FLOOD

COMMON ACRONYMS
A guide to acronyms commonly used throughout the book is below. For more information about the Halo Universe, please visit Halo Waypoint (halowaypoint.com).
B5D: Beta-5 Division
FSC: Flood Super Cell
MAC: Magnetic Accelerator Cannon
NMPD: New Mombasa Police Department
ODST: Orbital Drop Shock Troopers
SOEIV: Single Occupant Exoatmospheric Insertion Vessel
SWC: Special Warfare Center
UNSC: United Nations Space Command
VAS: Vestol Armor Systems
WST: Weapon System Technology

AIR ASSAULT ARMOR
MJOLNIR POWERED ASSAULT ARMOR/AA—AIR ASSAULT

The Air Assault [AA] customization of MJOLNIR armor was introduced into the line of Mark IV variants in 2535. In late 2551, an improved variant once again resurfaced with Mark V.

Mk. V—UA/CNM-AA

Jump Jet restraint

STATISTICS

HALO: REACH

In Halo: Reach's Armory, the Air Assault helmet costs 15,000 credits and requires the rank of Warrant Officer.

SERIES: Mark IV/Mark V
MANUFACTURER: Ushuaia Armory
TESTING SITE: Siófok Firing Range

ODST FAMILIARITY

The Air Assault helmet's resemblance to the older ODST models is not coincidental. It is believed that Ushuaia's substantial work with the Marine Corps BDU bled into their design for this armor.

Spartan Kat-B320 used Air Assault with Mark V armor when facing the Covenant threat on Reach.

AIRBORNE ADVANTAGE

Designed and produced by Siófok's Ushuaia Armory in 2535, the Air Assault armor variant was developed for the UNSC Army's airborne division. Offering specialized optics and heads-up display intel such as real-time satellite imagery and enemy signature allocation, this variant offered Spartans key advantages when being deployed in airborne scenarios.

STATISTICS

HALO 2 • HALO 3

The Albatross can be seen on two multiplayer maps: Halo 2's "Relic" and Halo 3's "Sandtrap."

MANUFACTURER: Ushuaia Armory
DESIGNATION: D96 Troop Carrier, Equipment Dropship
CREW: 1 pilot + 1 to 2 crew + 45 to 50 passengers
LENGTH: 120.8ft (36.8m)
WIDTH: 63.2ft (19.3m)

The Albatross is one of the UNSC's primary modes of long-range matériel deployment, transporting troops, equipment, and vehicles across large distances. Its significance on the battlefield is unquestioned.

D82-EST DARTER

The D82-EST, or "Darter," is another dropship similar to the Albatross that specializes in the transportation of base supplies.

Propulsion system

Cockpit

Cargo bay

The Albatross was used to bring 75 children deep into the Highland Wilderness during a SPARTAN-II training operation.

EQUIPMENT DEPLOYMENT

The D96-TCE Albatross has, for many decades, been an indispensible part of the UNSC's fleet of vehicles, capable of deploying equipment deep behind enemy lines from both atmospheric and exoatmospheric locations. Although this dropship is not typically armed, its nimble maneuverability and heavily armored, expansive cargo bay allow it to transport troops, weapons, and vehicles safely.

ALPHA HALO
INSTALLATION 04

One hundred millennia ago, the Forerunners designed an array of ringworlds, collectively called Halo, to destroy the merciless Flood. Alpha Halo was the first to be discovered by humanity.

Diameter:
6,214 miles
(10,000km)

DEDICATED STEWARD

As the Monitor of Alpha Halo, 343 Guilty Spark was an AI who maintained the ringworld. When it was destroyed, he devotedly continued his fight against the Flood until his own undoing.

STATISTICS

HALO: COMBAT EVOLVED • HALO 2 • HALO 3

Installation 04 is the centerpiece of Halo: Combat Evolved and it defines the Halo experience for many fans.

NAME: Installation 04
STAR: Soell
GRAVITY ANCHOR: Threshold/Basis
ADJACENT SATELLITE(S): Basis
GRAVITY: 0.992 G (approx)
ATMOSPHERE: 1 (N_2, O_2)
SURFACE TEMPERATURE: −9°F to 104°F (−23°C to 40°C) (controlled)

Surface width:
198 miles
(318km)

DISCOVERY OF HALO

On September 19, 2552, humanity stumbled upon Alpha Halo, one of the Forerunners' installations designed to wipe out all sentient life in order to obliterate the deadly Flood. When the Covenant unwittingly released the Flood onto the ring, the Master Chief was forced to destroy it by detonating the UNSC *Pillar of Autumn*'s fusion reactors. The ring's destruction triggered the Ark to forge a replacement Installation 04. Months later, the Chief destroyed this partially constructed ring, but this time he fired it in order to permanently quell the Flood.

Alpha Halo had an incredible plethora of flora and fauna, as well as a wide variety of environments for them to thrive in.

STATISTICS

HALO: REACH

Anchor 9 is a location in Halo: Reach's "Long Night of Solace," a mission which marks the introduction of space combat in a Halo title.

DESIGNATION: Anchor 9, UNSC Navy
LOCATION: Orbiting Reach
PRIMARY PURPOSE: Services, repairs, and refits ships for the UNSC Navy
CONFIDENTIAL PURPOSE: Rendezvous point for Operation: UPPER CUT

One of many service, repair, and refit stations orbiting Reach, Anchor 9 has three main hubs, each with its own docking bay and repair station. The platform can operate on various vessels, such as cruisers and frigates.

Frigate under repair

Docking bay

Point defense guns

As the largest UNSC shipyard, Reach held eighteen repair and refit stations in its orbit, including Anchor 9.

CRITICAL STATION

During the Covenant's invasion of the human planet Reach, Anchor 9 became a key military site. The station was used for Operation: UPPER CUT, a joint operation where the UNSC Army and Navy used a Shaw-Fujikawa Translight Engine as an improvised bomb to blow up the Covenant supercarrier, *Long Night of Solace*, above Reach. During this mission, a Sabre strike team was tasked with the defense of Anchor 9 against a Covenant assault. Though the orbital platform survived this attack unscathed, it was destroyed by a vast Covenant support fleet which arrived only days later.

ANDERS
PROFESSOR ELLEN ANDERS, PH.D.

A young civilian scientist renowned for her study of alien life forms, Professor Ellen Anders was abducted by ONI in 2531. She served as an incredible resource against the Covenant, albeit only for a short time.

The UNSC declared the *Spirit of Fire* and its crew, including Anders, to be "lost with all hands" on February 10, 2534.

RESEARCHER

Much like Dr. Catherine Halsey, Anders was requisitioned by ONI as a civilian consultant, having become particularly important when the Covenant's reign of terror slung itself across the Outer Colonies. In 2531, she was sent by ONI to the UNSC *Spirit of Fire*, where she investigated the Covenant's interest in structures of non-human origin buried below the surface of Harvest. After the *Spirit* pursued the Covenant to Arcadia, Anders was abducted by the Arbiter and brought to a Forerunner shield world where she was forced to activate an ancient fleet. Shortly after, the *Spirit of Fire*'s crew recovered her and together they developed a plan to stop the Covenant. This plan, however, left them stranded in the outer reaches of space and without any slipspace drive to get them back home. Anders' ultimate fate remains a mystery.

XENOBIOLOGIST

Anders studied theoretical xenobiology (the biology of aliens). Her research examined sites like Sigma Octanus, Bliss, and even the highly classified Onyx site, whose existence was denied by ONI.

IQ of 180

Arcadian clothing

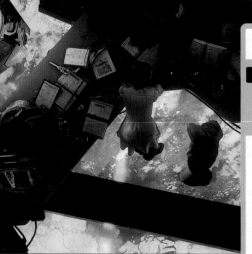

STATISTICS

HALO WARS

With Anders, players are able to use the Gremlin and the Hawk in Halo Wars' multiplayer.

FULL NAME: Ellen Anders
SERVICE NUMBER: CC-500493
BRANCH: UNSC Navy
GROUP: Office of Naval Intelligence, Section Three
HEIGHT: 5ft 10in (177.7cm)
WEIGHT: 114lbs (51.7kg)
HOMEWORLD: Arcadia
DATE OF BIRTH: August 13, 2503

ANTI-AIR WRAITH
TYPE-52 ANTI-AIRCRAFT ARTILLERY

STATISTICS

HALO 3 • HALO 3: ODST

Players can actually take control of the Anti-Air Wraith in Halo 3 through some fancy in-game footwork.

MANUFACTURER: Assembly Forges
DESIGNATION: Type-52 Anti-Aircraft Artillery
CREW: 1 driver + 1 gunner
LENGTH: 29.3ft (8.9m)
WIDTH: 30.3ft (9.2m)
PRIMARY ARMAMENT: Fuel Rod Cannon (2)
SECONDARY ARMAMENT: Medium Plasma Cannon

Despite its classification as an anti-aircraft artillery vehicle, the Anti-Air Wraith is a simple variation on the T-26 Wraith with a pair of heavy fuel rod weapons as an impressive anti-aircraft measure.

Plasma Cannon

Operator hatch

Heavy Fuel Rod Cannons

UPGRADED AMMUNITION

Most fuel rod weapons fire Class-2 ammunition, which is sufficient against infantry and armor within a short range, but it does not meet the longer distance demands of anti-aircraft combat. For this reason, the T-52 uses Class-3 ammunition.

Rear stabilizer

DOMINANT ARTILLERY

For the Covenant's family of Wraith vehicles, mobile ground control is only part of the equation. The Anti-Air Wraith provides the other part: mobile domination of the air. Each T-52 Wraith is fitted with twin fuel rod cannons that fire Class-3 fuel rods, capable of tracking the heat signatures of airborne vehicles. Anti-Air Wraiths are deployed in areas where the limitations of time or environment prevent the establishment of traditional anti-aircraft weaponry, or simply to mitigate the general lack of mobility present in anti-aircraft artillery like the T-27 Mantis or T-38 Tyrant.

ARBITER
RIPA 'MORAMEE

Prior to contact with humanity, Ripa 'Moramee served in the Ministry of Preservation, quelling internal uprisings with ruthless efficiency. He would later be called upon to fight against the humans on Harvest.

STATISTICS

HALO WARS

In the game Halo Wars, the Arbiter (as a hero) can activate "Rage Mode," which allows him impressive resilience and destructive potential.

FULL NAME: Ripa 'Moramee
SPECIES: Sangheili
RANK: Arbiter
MINISTRY: Ministry of Resolution
FLEET: Fleet of Glorious Interdiction
HEIGHT: 8ft 1in (246.3cm)
WEIGHT: 382lbs (173.3kg)
HOMEWORLD: Decided Heart
DATE OF BIRTH: June 2, 2478
DATE OF DEATH: February 25, 2531

Elaborate sallet

Customized hilt guard

Ready swordsman posture

RUTHLESS WARRIOR

After quelling a Grunt uprising and the heretical efforts of the Jackal known as Krith, Ripa 'Moramee took it upon himself to lead a coup d'état against the kaidon (leader) of Moram, but this led to his imprisonment. A short time later, however, the newly appointed High Prophet of Regret pardoned him so he could serve in the Fleet of Glorious Interdiction where, as Arbiter, he led a brutal campaign against the humans. This battle brought him to the ancient shield world and its Forerunner fleet, but in the process of activating this power, his forces were struck down, and he was killed by the human Sergeant John Forge.

The State of Moram was a Sangheili familial province located in the craggy atolls of the Elites' fortress world, Decided Heart.

ARBITER
THEL 'VADAM

STATISTICS

HALO 2 • HALO 3

In Halo 2, players can play as the Arbiter in certain missions, while in Halo 3, only the second player during a cooperative session can play as him.

FULL NAME: Thel 'Vadam (previously 'Vadamee)
SPECIES: Sangheili
RANK: Arbiter
PREVIOUS MINISTRY:
Ministry of Resolution
PREVIOUS FLEET:
Fleet of Particular Justice
HEIGHT: 7ft 10in (238.6cm)
WEIGHT: 319lbs (144.7kg)
HOMEWORLD: Sanghelios
DATE OF BIRTH:
December 10, 2485

When Alpha Halo was destroyed, Thel 'Vadam was punished and later given the role of Arbiter. The High Prophets hoped that this would lead to his end, but it brought civil war and ultimately the demise of the Covenant.

Thel's surname was 'Vadamee, the "ee" indicating devotion and service to the Covenant; something he relinquished during the Great Schism.

THE ROLE OF ARBITER

The Arbiter was once a position of great regard, but it became a mantle of self-sacrifice for redemption after an Arbiter from generations past brought incredible shame upon it.

Porous underarmor

HERETIC TO HERO

During the battle for the human military outpost Reach, Thel 'Vadam, the Supreme Commander of the Fleet of Particular Justice, pursued an enemy ship to a remote portion of the galaxy and arrived at Halo. His efforts to protect the ring failed and the Prophets, in response, punished him by giving him the sacrificial mantle of the Arbiter. But when the Prophets moved against the Elites, initiating the Great Schism, he turned against the Covenant, and fought alongside humanity. He helped to bring about the destruction of the Covenant and the Flood, and ultimately forged a tentative bond between the Elites and humans.

Near-ward ready stance

11

ARCADIA
PROCYON IV

Based in the Procyon system, Arcadia was a colony world covered in dense, largely unexplored forests and jungles. The world was peaceful until it was ripped apart by the Covenant's brutal war machine six years into the war.

Diameter:
8,090 miles
(13,019km)

STATISTICS

HALO WARS

There are three missions in Halo Wars set on Arcadia: "Arcadia City," "Arcadia Outskirts," and "Dome of Light."

STAR, POSITION: Procyon, IV
SATELLITE(S): Gihon, Pishon
GRAVITY: 1.02 G (approx)
ATMOSPHERE: 1.3 (N_2O_2)
SURFACE TEMPERATURE: 37°F to 98.6°F (3°C to 37°C)
DATE FOUNDED: 2429
MAJOR CITIES: Abaskun, Daylam, Pirth, Saqsin
POPULATION: 2,998,230 (pre-war)
SPACE TETHERS: 3

Arcadia has six continents: Avalon, Caledonia, Eire, Lemuria, Mu, and Pacifica.

FATE OF A PLANET

For many years, Arcadia was the definition of a thriving human colony, but in 2531 the Covenant struck, laying siege to the world in search of a Forerunner relic. After finding their prize near a UNSC military site, the Covenant forces unexpectedly departed for a shield world in a remote region of space. In the wake of this devastating attack, the planet was thrown into chaos, and its surviving population fell into anarchy. The Covenant returned in 2549 to wipe out the remaining human presence and finish what they had started two decades earlier.

ARDENT PRAYER

FLEET OF VALIANT PRUDENCE

Like other SDV-class corvettes, *Ardent Prayer* can carry a number of Seraph fighters, locked onto the ceiling of its primary bay.

Although the *Ardent Prayer* was part of a corvette contingent sent to subvert Reach's planetary defenses, it was used against the Covenant in the daring UNSC operation known as "UPPER CUT."

Command center

Landing platform

STATISTICS

HALO: REACH

Ardent Prayer appears throughout Halo: Reach's various game modes in "Long Night of Solace" (Campaign), "Corvette" (Firefight), and "Zealot" (multiplayer).

CLASS: SDV (Heavy Corvette)
FLEET: Fleet of Valiant Prudence
SHIPMASTER: Ardo 'Moretumee
LENGTH: 3,135ft (956m)
BEAM: 1,309ft (399m)
PRIMARY ARMAMENT:
Plasma Cannons

CAPTURED CORVETTE

The *Ardent Prayer* was a heavy corvette primarily used for survey and light troop deployment—roles it carried out during the Covenant's invasion of Reach. On August 14, 2552, the *Ardent Prayer* was attacked by a UNSC Sabre strike force and their escort frigate, the UNSC *Savannah*. This assault took out its engines, allowing the human forces to board it and take full control. They eventually used it to bring a makeshift bomb within proximity of the Valiant Prudence's flagship, the supercarrier *Long Night of Solace*. The subsequent detonation completely obliterated both the *Ardent Prayer* and the *Solace*.

Well beyond the periphery of the Milky Way galaxy, the Ark is the foundry where the Halo installations were created. The Ark also gave selected species protection from the Halo rings in the event that they were fired.

STATISTICS

HALO 3

In the Halo 3 mission "The Ark," the UNSC finally arrives at this enormous superstructure, which becomes the final battle site of the Covenant War.

NAME: Installation 00
GRAVITY: 1G
ATMOSPHERE: 1.0 (N_2, O_2, Ar)
SURFACE TEMPERATURE: –22°F to 122°F (–30°C to 50°C)

Interior surface

Diameter: 79,243 miles (127,530km)

The Ark can only be reached using a Forerunner keyship to activate a gateway Portal buried on specific planets in the galaxy.

Raw materials mine

Halo forging site

CONSERVATION MEASURE

The Forerunners used the Ark as part of the Conservation Measure—an effort which extracted and relocated specific species from across the galaxy onto the installation's surface in order to prevent the complete eradication of all sentient life forms when the Halo Array fired.

ANCIENT REFUGE

Approximately one hundred thousand years before humanity fought the Covenant above the Ark, the Forerunners used this massive machine to forge a number of ringworlds—the Halo Array. The Ark was meant to be a refuge from the Flood and the Array itself. At the end of the war with the Covenant, the UNSC followed their enemies to this remote construct, prevented them from firing Halo, and used a newly formed replacement ring of Installation 04 to obliterate the extant Flood population and the Ark itself.

ARMOR ABILITIES
COMBAT ENHANCEMENT ARMOR MODULES

STATISTICS

HALO: REACH

Halo: Reach multiplayer was the first game to present "Loadouts," which offer players the ability to select different armor abilities when respawning in both multiplayer and Firefight game modes.

TYPES:
Active Camouflage
Armor Lock
Drop Shield
Evade
Holographic Decoy
Jet Pack
Sprint

Armor abilities are enhancement mechanisms in the base of a super-soldier's armored back. These upgrades range from increased speed and protection to flight and Holographic Decoys.

Jet Pack

Armor abilities are temporary but rechargeable enhancements.

Armor Lock

Armor Lock

Sprint

SPECIALIZED UPGRADES

UNSC and Covenant armor both offer customized attachments that tweak the armor's performance of specific functions or synchronize separate hardware with the armor for entirely new functionality. For Spartans, these alterations are synced with the soldier's neural network to improve MJOLNIR's performance. In some cases, new physical components are added such as thrusters for the jet pack or refractive sensors for active camouflage. This effect has not been fully explored within Covenant technology, though evidence supports the theory that both Elite and Brute armor carry a similar system of dummy modules or terminator plugs.

ASSAULT RIFLE
MA INDIVIDUAL COMBAT WEAPON SYSTEM

The Assault Rifle represents an array of Individual Combat Weapon Systems with the model prefix "MA." It is the most commonly issued weapon of the UNSC, instantly recognizable due to its accentuated and bulky shroud.

The MA37 Individual Combat Weapon System was first introduced into the UNSC in 2437.

Ammo counter

Barrel shroud

Stock

Grip

AMMUNITION OPTIONS
The magazine capacity for the Assault Rifle varies. However, it is usually 32 or 60 rounds, depending on the model.

STANDARD-ISSUE RIFLE

The Assault Rifle is an air-cooled, gas-operated, magazine-fed rifle, which fires 7.62 x 51mm rounds. It is automatic and has reasonable range but quickly loses accuracy over longer distances. Rather than a single line of weapons, the MA ICWS represents a vast arrangement of firearms, the most popular of which are the MA2B, MA3, MA37, MA5B, MA5C, and MA5K. All vary incrementally from model to model, but most share the same basic design and functionality. Presently, the UNSC Marine Corps uses the MA5B and MA5C models, whereas the UNSC Army utilizes the MA37.

Dot was crucial during Operation: UPPER CUT, where she led Noble Five and Noble Six to a corvette to destroy the supercarrier *Long Night of Solace*.

The UNSC AI construct Auntie Dot served as intelligence support and liaison between Command and the Special Warfare group known as Noble Team, assisting with on-the-fly intel and mission objectives.

Communication pattern

STATISTICS

HALO: REACH

Dot's physical holographic manifestation, a property typical to all AI constructs, is never seen in the Halo games.

SERIAL NUMBER: ADT 6849-9
ORIGIN: UNSC Army
CLASS: Dumb Artificial Intelligence
ROLE: Intelligence Support
ACTIVATION DATE: May 9, 2541

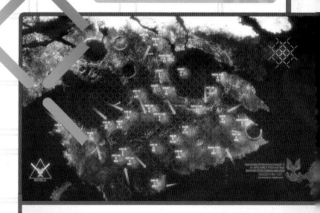

COMMAND LIAISON

Although Auntie Dot is considered a "dumb" Artificial Intelligence, her field of expertise, while relatively narrow, still outstrips the comprehension capacity of most humans. Specializing in operative military intelligence, Dot served as field liaison between Colonel Urban Holland and Noble Team. She provided crucial data during Noble's actions against the Covenant across the surface of Reach.
It is well known that the planet eventually fell to the Covenant, but Dot's fate remains a mystery.

INTELLIGENCE SUPPORT

Dot's comparatively cold tone and flat demeanor is characteristic of some "dumb" AI constructs. They are considered to be an important facet of intelligence support in the field.

Lacks holographic form

BANSHEE
TYPE-26 GROUND SUPPORT AIRCRAFT

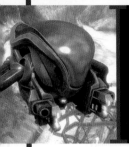

The T-26 Banshee is easily the most recognizable Covenant in-atmosphere combat aircraft. While it is only lightly armored, its mobility and arsenal make it an important asset in the Covenant's ground support measures.

Fuel Rod Cannon

Cockpit

Canard aileron

Plasma Cannon

The architecture on any T-26 varies depending on the line and year it was manufactured, as well as the branch in which it is used.

FORMIDABLE FLOCKS

A single flier is easily brought down in battle, but when Banshees strike in groups they pose a significant threat to ground forces.

EFFECTIVE SUPPORT

The Type-26 Ground Support Aircraft, also known as the Banshee, is like other Covenant vehicles in that it varies aesthetically from one branch to another. Most Banshees use twin plasma cannons as well as a single forward-mounted heavy fuel rod cannon. Its core functionality and purpose—providing air support to ground forces—has remained largely unchanged for decades. Plainly speaking, Banshees provide infantry with both eyes in the sky and an airborne arsenal to resolve ground-based threats if deemed necessary.

BANSHEE FIGHTER
TYPE-27 EXOATMOSPHERIC MULTI-ROLE FIGHTER

HALO: REACH

The UNSC has squared off against Banshee fighters in various campaigns throughout the Covenant War, most notably on Reach.

MANUFACTURER: Assembly Forges
DESIGNATION: Type-27
Exoatmospheric Multi-Role Fighter
CREW: 1 pilot
LENGTH: 35.7ft (10.9m)
WIDTH: 28.2ft (8.6m)
PRIMARY ARMAMENT:
Heavy Plasma Cannon (2)
SECONDARY ARMAMENT:
Fuel Rod Cannon

As a central part of the Covenant's exoatmospheric naval combat, Banshee fighters are deployed en masse in an effort to overwhelm and destroy enemy targets through numeric superiority.

Cockpit

Firing channel

Tail

Canard

Typically speaking, the Banshee fighter is only a significant threat to Sabre fighters when used in large numbers.

SPACE BANSHEES

T-27 Banshee fighters are oftentimes referred to as "Space Banshees" to distinguish them from T-26 Ground Support Aircraft.

VERSATILE SPACE FIGHTER

The Type-27 XMF is a multi-role fighter used primarily for quick and dirty strikes. In large numbers, it also provides a defensive line for interception, interference, and reinforcement. Unlike the T-26, the T-27 has undergone physical modifications to allow for operation in a vacuum. Apart from having an air-locked cockpit, the fighter's canards are swept forward and the tail is extended roughly two meters back for maneuverability. The heavy plasma cannon is similar to the T-26's, but its firing channel has been significantly extended for combat in space.

Since Halo: Combat Evolved, Battle Creek's squat, two-base layout, buried in the mysterious warrens of a Halo ring, has proven to be an incredibly versatile map, suiting the needs of both team and free-for-all gametypes.

STATISTICS

HALO: COMBAT EVOLVED • HALO 2

Although this map worked incredibly well with Slayer, it was also ideal for team-based objective gametypes like Capture the Flag and Assault.

ENVIRONMENT: Two bases within a ravine
RELEVANCE: Halo installation
LAYOUT: Small-scale symmetrical battlefield
PLAYER COUNT: 8 to 16
KEY WEAPONS: Sniper Rifle, Rocket Launcher

Battle Creek (Halo: CE)

Beaver Creek (Halo 2)

The purpose and function of the two structures on this Halo ringworld remain a mystery to this day.

CLASSIC BATTLEGROUND

Halo: Combat Evolved's Battle Creek, which later reappeared as Beaver Creek in Halo 2, is a small outdoor map located at the bottom of a truncated ravine with two bases at each end. Apart from the bases themselves, the map has a watery trench dividing both sides and a single arch that climbs up toward one of the walls and holds the Rocket Launcher. Opposite this is the Sniper Rifle, resting atop a cleft in the far wall. Behind each base is a teleporter offering swift transportation from one side of the map to the other. This map's design provided a template for many small, symmetrical Halo maps in the years which followed.

STATISTICS

HALO 2 • HALO 3

Though fictionally the Battle Rifle has three modes of fire, Halo games feature its most effective mode—a default three-round burst that is quite efficient at culling most Covenant infantry.

MANUFACTURER: Misriah Armory
SERIES: BR55HB Service Rifle
AMMUNITION: 9.5 x 40mm KURZ
SAP-HE (Semi-Armor Piercing, High Explosive)
MAGAZINE CAPACITY: 36 rounds (varies)
LENGTH: 45.6in (115.8cm)
FIRING MODE: Automatic, semi-automatic, burst

The Battle Rifle's default three-round burst is incredibly effective against energy-shielded enemies; a feature which has afforded it no small measure of popularity in the UNSC's war against the Covenant.

Scope

Ammo counter

36

Barrel

VARIETY IN THE FIELD

The standard BR55 Service Rifle is smaller than the heavy barrel variant at 35.4in (89.9cm), though it operates almost identically.

Pistol grip

The M392 DMR was pervasive throughout all branches of the UNSC for several decades until the BR55's popularity eclipsed it in 2548.

RANGED PRECISION

Accurate, precise, and efficient, the BR55HB SR represents one of the most well-established and favored arms in the entire UNSC. The weapon was originally prototyped for combat during the rebellion, though its robust stopping power and functionality made it extremely popular as humanity began to face the Covenant in the trenches. With 36 SAP-HE rounds per magazine and the default firing mode of three-burst, the Battle Rifle is considered by many to be the preeminent ranged combat weapon in the UNSC's arsenal.

BLOOD GULCH
HALO MULTIPLAYER MAP

Perhaps the most well-known of all the Halo maps, Blood Gulch from Halo: Combat Evolved became the precursor for large-scale multiplayer environments in all Halo titles that followed.

STATISTICS

HALO: COMBAT EVOLVED • HALO 2 HALO WARS • HALO: REACH

Blood Gulch is a versatile map, but the gametype most associated with it is Capture the Flag, where teams attempt to steal their opponent's flag while protecting their own.

ENVIRONMENT: Two bases within a canyon
RELEVANCE: Halo installation
LAYOUT: Large-scale symmetrical battlefield
PLAYER COUNT: 8 to 16
KEY WEAPONS: Sniper Rifle, Rocket Launcher, Pistol (Halo: CE), Battle Rifle (Halo 2), DMR (Halo: Reach)

A variation of Blood Gulch made a surprising but welcome appearance in the real-time strategy game Halo Wars.

Hemorrhage (Halo: Reach)

FAVORED BATTLEFIELD

A vast open canyon floor with rolling hills has entered the consciousness of Halo fans as the quintessential multiplayer environment. This is largely because of the success of Halo: Combat Evolved's Blood Gulch, as well as both Coagulation and Hemorrhage, which followed. With fortified bases on both sides of the canyon and an expansive battlefield between, Blood Gulch provided the foundation for both vehicular warfare and long-range combat in multiplayer and it lives on in Halo: Reach's Hemorrhage.

Blood Gulch (Halo: CE)

Coagulation (Halo 2)

STATISTICS

**HALO 2 • HALO 3 • HALO WARS
HALO 3: ODST • HALO: REACH**

The first chieftain to appear in a Halo game was Tartarus in Halo 2, though chieftains in general are more commonly seen in Halo 3, Halo 3: ODST, and in Halo: Reach.

SPECIES: Jiralhanae, *Servus ferox*
AVERAGE HEIGHT: 8ft 5in to 9ft 2in (259cm to 280cm)
AVERAGE WEIGHT: 1,125lbs to 1,500lbs (500kg to 680kg)
HOMEWORLD: Doisac

The Brutes' culture of pack rivalry, with a strong proclivity toward violence, relies on chieftains for its organization. These are alpha leaders who hold the highest political and familial status.

Ceremonial helmet

CHIEFTAIN OF THE BRUTES

The most notorious Brute chieftain was Tartarus, whose alignment with the High Prophet of Truth gave the Brutes full but short-lived control over the Covenant military.

Reinforced Chieftain armor

LEADER OF THE PACK

The role of chieftain was established long before the Covenant integrated the Brute species into their number, but such a mantle was encouraged in an effort to maintain an established order within their kind. The role is based on the Brutes' pack-centric sociology and their species' aggressive behavior, as each chieftain is killed and removed by their successor, which keeps the strongest members at the top of each pack and clan at all times.

Historically, the Brute war hammer is the most recognizable, totemistic symbol of a chieftain's power, although not every chieftain wields one.

BRUTE SHOT
TYPE-25 GRENADE LAUNCHER

Like other weapons originating from the Brutes, the Brute Shot is intended to terrify as much as it is to kill. Not only does the launcher fire explosive ordnance, but it also houses a deadly, guillotine-like blade.

STATISTICS

HALO 2 • HALO 3 • HALO WARS
HALO 3: ODST

In Halo 2, the Brute Shot has four grenades per magazine, while in Halo 3 it has a total of six grenades.

MANUFACTURER: Sacred Promissory
DESIGNATION: Type-25 Grenade Launcher
AMMUNITION: Fragmentation Grenade
MAGAZINE CAPACITY: 4 or 6 grenades
LENGTH: 72.4in (183.8cm)
FIRING MODE: Semi-automatic

SIMPLE AND DEADLY

As a testament to the weapon's lethal simplicity, the Brutes have used this grenade launcher for decades, even prior to their integration into the Covenant.

Firing grip

Despite this weapon's comparatively large size at six feet long, Brutes use it more like a rifle than a support weapon.

Stabilizing grip

Barrel

Blade

DEADLY LAUNCHER

The Type-25 Grenade Launcher is a Brute-crafted ballistic launcher capable of firing up to six fragmentation rounds at a target. Against unshielded infantry, the Brute Shot is extremely effective, and while it can't destroy a vehicle upon impact, it can easily knock one over, making its now unprotected passengers vulnerable. The predictable, though still frightening, element to the Brute Shot is the enormous blade mounted into the weapon's stock—yet another example of the species' merciless barbarity. The tungsten-alloy blade is easily capable of cutting through flesh, as the Brutes have exhaustively proven during the Covenant War.

BRUTES

STATISTICS

HALO 2 • HALO 3 • HALO WARS
HALO 3: ODST • HALO: REACH

The Brutes first appeared in Halo 2, although chronologically their appearances in Halo Wars and Halo: Reach precede Halo 2's events.

SPECIES: Jiralhanae, *Servus ferox*
AVERAGE HEIGHT: 8ft 5in to 9ft 2in (259cm to 280cm)
AVERAGE WEIGHT: 1,125lbs to 1,500lbs (500kg to 680kg)
HOMEWORLD: Doisac
TYPES/FORMS:
Minor, Major, Ultra, Stalker, Jumper, Bodyguard, Captain, Chieftain

For decades, the Brutes were militarily subordinate to the Elites, but when an opportunity to overthrow their leaders manifested, they exploited it without hesitation.

Captain helmet

Clan pauldron

Gravity hammer

The Brute homeworld, Doisac, is the third planet in the Oth Sonin system and is orbited by the triple moons of Soirapt, Teash, and Warial.

THE SAVAGES

On their homeworld of Doisac, the Brutes were rocked by a violent civil war that consumed their entire planet, reverting them to a pre-industrial state. In 2492, they made contact with Prophet missionaries and were quickly grafted into the Covenant, though the Elites suspected that such a savage civilization would bring about internal conflict. Those suspicions were proven true less than a century later when the High Prophet of Truth appointed the Brutes for his own security, proclaiming the Elites to be heretics deserving extermination. The resulting civil war threw the Covenant into turmoil and eventually brought about the alliance's bitter defeat above the surface of the Ark.

CLAN WARFARE

As made evident by their varying equipment and grooming practices, the Brute species still battled intertribal disunity, even after their incorporation into the Covenant.

BUCK

GUNNERY SERGEANT EDWARD BUCK

A career soldier and combat veteran, Gunnery Sergeant Eddie Buck saw his service come to a culmination with the arrival of the Covenant on Earth, when he and his squad were selected for a highly classified operation.

ODST-CNM

STATISTICS

HALO 3: ODST • HALO: REACH

Players are dropped into the boots of Eddie Buck in Halo 3: ODST's "Tayari Plaza," where they begin to unravel the mystery of New Mombasa.

FULL NAME: Edward Buck
SERVICE NUMBER: 92458-37017-EB
BRANCH: UNSC Marine Corps
GROUP: Naval Special Weapons, Orbital Drop Shock Troopers
RANK: Gunnery Sergeant
HEIGHT: 6ft 2in (188cm)
WEIGHT: 196lbs (89kg)
HOMEWORLD: Draco III
DATE OF BIRTH: August 22, 2510

MA5C Assault Rifle

In 2545 when the Covenant attacked Buck's homeworld, Draco III, they gathered together and mercilessly executed much of its population.

ODST BDU

THE FALL OF REACH

During the Covenant's siege of New Alexandria on Reach, Buck was escorted by Noble Six on a top-secret mission over the city's skyline.

DEDICATED LEADER

Enlisting in the UNSC Marine Corps in 2528, Edward Buck served for over two decades in the war against the Covenant, eventually establishing himself as an incredibly dedicated leader among the Orbital Drop Shock Troopers. On October 20, 2552, when the Covenant tried to gain footing in the African city of New Mombasa, Buck led a squad of replacements into the heart of the city in search of an ONI-designated Tier One asset. Despite the squad being scattered upon entry, Buck searched for and found each teammate, secured the asset, and succeeded in his mission.

STATISTICS

HALO 2

As the Master Chief, players defend this platform in the Halo 2 mission "Cairo Station."

DESIGNATION: OWP-142/Orbital Weapon Platform Array-142
HEIGHT: 4,383 (1,336m)
WIDTH: 2,580 (786m)
ARMAMENT: Mark V MAC

Cairo Station is one of 300 Orbital Weapon Platforms set in geosynchronous orbit around Earth. It played an important role during the Covenant's invasion and occupation of the human homeworld.

Orbital platforms are built around an enormous fifth-generation "Super MAC"—a large-scale asynchronous linear induction weapon.

"Recreation" was the first room to see combat when the Covenant assaulted Cairo station.

Docked frigate

Bridge

Portside shipping

Hangar A-02

Hangar A-01

Recreation

EARTH'S LAST DEFENSE

Located within the same battle cluster as stations Athens and Malta, Cairo Station (OWP-142) was one of many weapon platforms which surrounded Earth in 2552. When the High Prophet of Regret first arrived on October 20, 2552, he tore through this cluster, sending advance boarding parties onto all three platforms and successfully destroying two. Only Cairo managed to survive, in large part due to the Master Chief, who pursued Regret all the way to Earth's surface. Despite an overwhelming Covenant occupation force, Cairo Station remained intact and under humanity's control throughout the invasion, serving as Lord Hood's base of operations until November 17, 2552.

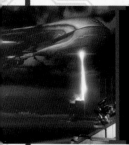

CARRIER
COVENANT SHIP CLASSIFICATION

One of the most prevalent of Covenant ships, carriers are critical in the capture and occupation of any targeted world, providing not only command and support, but overwhelming firepower.

A RARE SIGHT

CSO-class carriers, also known as "supercarriers," are incredibly rare. The most notable is the one that first struck Reach: the Covenant's *Long Night of Solace*.

Assault carriers are often used as flagships; lead vessels which serve as a fleet's command center.

STATISTICS

HALO 2 • HALO 3 • HALO 3: ODST HALO: REACH

CLASS: DDS (Carrier)
LENGTH: 9,843ft (3,000m)
BEAM: 3,891ft (1,186m)
USE: Occupation, force deployment

CLASS: CAS (Assault Carrier)
LENGTH: 17,541ft (5,347m)
BEAM: 6,948ft (2,118m)
USE: Attack, command

CLASS: CSO (Supercarrier)
LENGTH: 95,014ft (28,960m)
BEAM: 37,566ft (11,447m)
USE: Command, occupation support

PRIMARY ARMAMENT:
Ventral Cleansing Beam
SECONDARY ARMAMENT:
Anterior Plasma Cannons
TERTIARY ARMAMENT:
Point Laser Defense

Gravity lift

Modular dispersal breach

Ventral Cleansing Beam

COMMANDING THE FLEET

Most Covenant carriers can be categorized into three distinct classes, though they all share similar architecture and weaponry. The most common of the three is the CAS-class or "assault carrier," a stalwart part of the Covenant's offensive campaign for the last three decades. Although DDS-class and CSO-class ships appear less frequently, they are both similarly effective. If cruisers represent the Covenant fleet's general body mass, then carriers represent its head, offering command and operational support from a heavily armed and armored location.

CARTER
COMMANDER CARTER-A259, SPARTAN-III

STATISTICS

HALO: REACH

In Halo: Reach, players follow the command of Carter-A259 as they take the fight to the Covenant across the surface of Reach.

FULL NAME: Carter-A259
SERVICE NUMBER: S-A259
BRANCH: UNSC Army
GROUP: Special Warfare, Group Three
RANK: Commander
HEIGHT: 6ft 10in (208.3cm)
WEIGHT: 250lbs (113.4kg)
HOMEWORLD: Biko
DATE OF BIRTH: August 27, 2520
DATE OF DEATH: August 30, 2552

A veteran soldier of the SPARTAN-III project, Carter-A259 led Noble Team on many missions against the Covenant before finally making the ultimate sacrifice on the planet Reach.

Mk. V—Commando helmet

M392 DMR

Mk. V—Commando pauldron

FEARLESS COMMANDER

Abducted as a child and transported to the classified planet of Onyx where he trained in the SPARTAN-III project, Carter-A259 quickly displayed his skills as a leader. Some time later he was given the rank of commander on the Special Warfare team codenamed "Noble," where he served as their leader for a number of years. In July of 2552, his team was sent to Reach to investigate a possible rebel attack, not knowing that the true threat was the Covenant. Carter bravely led Noble against this enemy, defending the planet to the death.

Carter-A259 was part of Alpha Company, the first batch of soldiers to be generated by the top secret SPARTAN-III project.

CARTOGRAPHER
MAP FACILITY, FORERUNNER INSTALLATION

Located on various Forerunner installations, the Cartographer houses a map room containing a holographic schematic of the entire structure, its critical sites, and other essential data.

A distributed intelligence can access the map room console and generate waypoint indicators on the holographic superstructure.

HALO'S ATLAS

When the Forerunners began designing artificial worlds they saw the need for a facility which would provide a real-time map of each installation, along with other relevant information as directed by the user. While there is no set architectural template for the Cartographer facilities, those which exist on Halo installations are typically large building structures that house a variety of compartments and rooms, one of which is the map room. Cartographers are important to most Forerunner superstructures, since the installations themselves are enormous and contain many critical sites separated by immense distances.

BEHIND LOCKED DOORS

The map room, like many other facilities on Forerunner installations, is protected by a variety of powerful security measures.

STATISTICS

HALO: COMBAT EVOLVED • HALO 3

In the Halo 3 Campaign mission "The Ark," the player has to penetrate Installation 00's walled-off interior in order to access the Cartographer.

DESIGNATION: Map Facility of a Forerunner installation
SITES: Forerunner installations
FUNCTION: Provides a holographic, real-time map of the installation
COMPOSITION: A building with centralized map room within

CHOPPER
TYPE-25 RAPID ASSAULT VEHICLE

STATISTICS

HALO 3 • HALO WARS • HALO 3: ODST

Boosting through enemy infantry and vehicles is an easy and effective tactic with the Covenant's Chopper.

MANUFACTURER: Sacred Promissory
DESIGNATION: Type-25 Rapid Assault Vehicle
CREW: 1 operator
LENGTH: 20.9ft (6.4m)
WIDTH: 9.3ft (2.8m)
PRIMARY ARMAMENT:
35mm Autocannon (4)
SECONDARY ARMAMENT: Ramming Targe

Although the Chopper was originally designed for amicable purposes, the Brutes reconfigured it to meet their needs, adding a formidable arsenal and transforming the machine into a swift and violent assault vehicle.

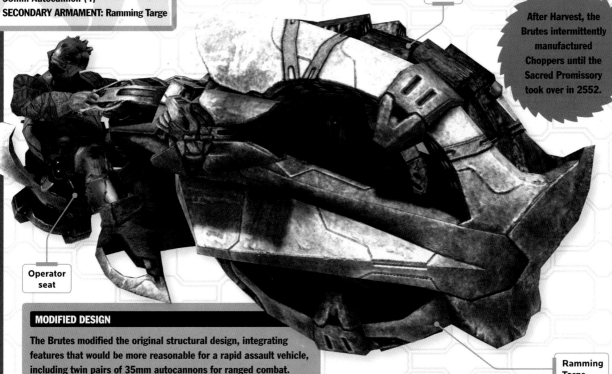

Wheel

After Harvest, the Brutes intermittently manufactured Choppers until the Sacred Promissory took over in 2552.

Operator seat

Ramming Targe

MODIFIED DESIGN

The Brutes modified the original structural design, integrating features that would be more reasonable for a rapid assault vehicle, including twin pairs of 35mm autocannons for ranged combat.

VICIOUS ARMAMENT

Shortly before the Brute cruiser *Rapid Conversion* made contact with humanity on the planet Harvest, an accident damaged one of the Spirit dropships onboard. A Covenant Engineer, *Lighter Than Some*, seized this opportunity to atone for a past misdeed against the humans. Using the Spirit's parts, the Engineer created a new pair of vehicles, akin to Harvest's JOTUN tractors, as a gift. Believing these to be combat vehicles, the Brutes aboard the cruiser affixed weapons to the machines, deploying them against the very same humans for whom they were intended.

COBRA
SPECIAL PURPOSE-42 MAIN BATTLE TANK

The Cobra is a self-propelled heavy weapon platform designed to fire slugs at supersonic speeds that can penetrate and disable enemy targets in a single shot. Its mobile and lockdown modes both provide devastating results.

M98 LRG
(stowed)

SP-42 MBTs first saw action in 2497, when they were employed during the course of Operation: CHARLEMAGNE.

Retractable rear wheels

Extendable stabilizer

MOBILITY OPTIMIZED

For speed and mobility, the Cobra eschews the tread design typical of most tanks, and utilizes six rugged all-terrain wheels.

Pivoting wheel guard

SPECIALIZED FIREPOWER

The Cobra is an anti-matériel/anti-fortification tank with twin M66 LRGs. When facing other vehicles or minor fortifications, it operates in mobile mode, allowing the tank to manuever and attack simultaneously. When the vehicle is in lockdown mode, it becomes stationary, stowing its M66 LRGs and allowing the heavier M98 to emerge. From a fixed position, this weapon can fire a 105mm slug at supersonic speeds and is ideal for use against heavily fortified structures.

UNSC

COMMANDO ARMOR
MJOLNIR POWERED ASSAULT ARMOR/K—COMMANDO

STATISTICS

HALO: REACH

The Commando helmet is available in Halo: Reach's Armory for 85,000 credits with the rank of Commander.

SERIES: Mark IV/Mark V
MANUFACTURER: Chalybs Defense Solutions
TESTING SITE: Chalybs Testing Preserve

The Commando variant of MJOLNIR armor is a modification of the standard Mark IV, designed to improve a Spartan's tactical awareness on the battlefield. Its success led to the Mark V upgrade in late 2551.

Mk. V—K/ HUL

SIEGE OF THE INNER COLONIES

Commando was an armor variant worn frequently by both **SPARTAN-II** and **SPARTAN-III** super-soldiers during the Siege of the Inner Colonies.

Mk. V—Commando pauldron

MA5C Assault Rifle

Field support attachment

Carter-A259, commander of the legendary Noble Team, used a modified version of the MJOLNIR/K during the battle for the planet Reach.

TACTICAL PACKAGE

Most of the Commando's features can be modularly applied to standard Mark IV/Mark V MJOLNIR platforms, but the Commando package offers the most comprehensive collection of tactical hardware and systems. The suite includes command network modules, third-generation uplink capabilities, and an assortment of tactical/logistical field solutions. This allows Spartans to access and process mission intel at an unparalleled level of detail, even while engaged with hostile forces.

CONCUSSION RIFLE
TYPE-50 DIRECTED ENERGY RIFLE/HEAVY

The short-range Concussion Rifle is one of the Covenant's many munitions-launching infantry weapons. It is semi-automatic and is typically carried by the Covenant's higher-ranking soldiers.

STATISTICS

HALO: REACH

A wise tactic in Halo: Reach's multiplayer is to use the Concussion Rifle to knock over an enemy-controlled vehicle, exposing the crew and passengers to direct weapon fire.

MANUFACTURER: Merchants of Qikost
DESIGNATION: Type-50 Directed Energy Rifle/Heavy
AMMUNITION: Concussive Explosive Plasma
MAGAZINE CAPACITY: 6 units
LENGTH: 40.5in (103cm)
FIRING MODE: Semi-automatic

The Merchants of Qikost manufacture this and other weapons of Elite heritage that predate the formation of the Covenant.

Housing

Stock

Grip

SANGHEILI DESIGN

The T-50 Concussion Rifle has been around longer than the Brute's T-25 and the human's M319 grenade launchers, though it was observed by humanity only late into the war.

POWERFUL RIFLE

Capable of firing six rounds of explosive plasma, the Concussion Rifle is based on the same plasma technology used in medium to heavy cannons, and it closely resembles the mortar systems employed by both Wraiths and Revenants. Against enemy infantry, it is incredibly effective; against enemy vehicles, it causes significant damage over time, but more importantly, it can overturn a vehicle, spilling its contents and passengers. This weapon is linked to specific ranks, as it requires specialized training due to the hazards the rifle can pose when misused.

CONTROL ROOM

CONTROL CENTER, FORERUNNER INSTALLATION

STATISTICS

**HALO: COMBAT EVOLVED
HALO 2 • HALO 3 • HALO WARS**

One of the most popular missions in all of Halo is the first game's "Assault on the Control Room," where the player must storm an enormous citadel to reach Installation 04's control center.

DESIGNATION: Control Center of a Forerunner installation
SITES: Forerunner installations
FUNCTION: Activation, control, and management of an installation
COMPOSITION: Heavily guarded citadel or fortification, cavernous main chamber

A control room is the central facility on any Forerunner installation. It offers the user control over a number of systems including maintenance, manufacturing, weather, and most importantly, its key weapon.

THE INDEX

Activating the Halo rings requires a key called the Index, a slender, Forerunner-crafted object which must be reunited with the core system to initiate Halo's defenses.

ACTIVATION CHAMBER

Despite the fact that a control center can perform numerous operations across the vast Forerunner superstructure on which it resides, its primary function is the initiation of whatever weapon system the installation might have. For the Halo rings, this means the firing of the Array; for a shield world, it could mean the activation of a Forerunner fleet or some other hidden weapon. In all known cases, the activation inexorably requires a human or "Reclaimer" in order to be actualized.

CORTANA

CTN 0452-9

Dr. Catherine Halsey cloned her own brain to create ONI's artificial intelligence "Cortana." She hoped that this AI, having unequalled functionality and capability, would help to achieve her goal for the SPARTAN-II program.

Holographic representation

ILLEGAL ORIGIN

By cloning herself to create Cortana, Dr. Catherine Halsey knowingly broke civilian law, UNSC military regulations, and UN Colonial Mortal Dictata.

AIs like Cortana have an operational lifespan of seven years, after which they can fall prey to the terminal condition known as "rampancy."

A CRITICAL ASSET

Cortana was originally designed in 2549 for Operation: RED FLAG. Her mission was to aid the Spartans in the infiltration of a Covenant vessel and the capture of one of their Prophets. When that mission was derailed by the invasion of Reach, Cortana and the Spartan entrusted with her safekeeping, Master Chief John-117, fled the planet and found their way to Halo. Cortana and the Chief experienced this new alien world and its secrets, forging a strong bond in the process. Their discovery would eventually pave the way for humanity's victory.

STATISTICS

HALO: COMBAT EVOLVED
HALO 2 • HALO 3 • HALO: REACH

Cortana's central role within the Halo Trilogy was initiated when players took the role of the Master Chief in Halo: Combat Evolved.

SERIAL NUMBER: CTN 0452-9
ORIGIN: Office of Naval Intelligence, Dr. Catherine Halsey
CLASS: Smart Artificial Intelligence
ROLE: Software Infiltration
ACTIVATION DATE: November 7, 2549

STATISTICS

HALO: REACH

In the Halo: Reach mission "Long Night of Solace," players battle their way through a Covenant corvette named *Ardent Prayer*.

CLASS: DAV (Light Corvette)
LENGTH: 1,590ft (485m)
BEAM: 985ft (202m)
USE: Stealth, information gathering

CLASS: SDV (Heavy Corvette)
LENGTH: 3,135ft (956m)
BEAM: 1,309ft (399m)
USE: Interference, force deployment

ARMAMENT: Heavy Plasma Cannons

Covenant corvettes are fast, sleek, and very efficient at infiltrating a planet's defenses. Despite limited weaponry, their infantry transport and deployment capacities make them a vital element of Covenant occupation.

Landing platform

Corvettes rarely engage in ship-to-ship combat. Instead they employ fighters to battle enemies and allow the main ship to escape.

Command center

BATTLE FOR REACH

Early on during the battle for the planet Reach, the Covenant used the sleek SDV-class corvettes to launch both air and ground assaults against specific UNSC targets.

SWIFT AND SILENT

Corvettes within the Covenant's vast naval resources usually take part in advanced surveying of reliquary sites; their size, maneuverability, and stealth measures allow them to remain undetected in most cases. There is evidence of several types of Covenant corvettes, but two classes have been encountered most often: DAV (Light Corvette) and SDV (Heavy Corvette). The smaller and more nimble DAV-class corvette has the ability to cloak itself and transmit data from a planet's surface, whereas the SDV-class is more often associated with troop deployment.

COVENANT CARBINE
TYPE-51 CARBINE

The Covenant Carbine is a recoil-operated, semi-automatic, charger-fed marksman rifle capable of firing 8 x 60mm ballistic rounds accurately at a target up to six hundred meters away.

STATISTICS

HALO 2 • HALO 3 • HALO 3: ODST

The Covenant Carbine is particularly useful in Halo 3: ODST, in which it fulfils the role of a mid-to-long range marksman rifle.

MANUFACTURER: Iruiru Armory
DESIGNATION: Type-51 Carbine
AMMUNITION: 8 x 60mm Caseless Radioactive Round
MAGAZINE CAPACITY: 18 rounds
LENGTH: 50in (127.1cm)
FIRING MODE: Semi-automatic

LETHAL DOSAGE

The caseless 8 x 60mm radioactive rounds are without a doubt deadly. Upon impact, they release toxic material into a victim's bloodstream, which can kill within a matter of minutes if not treated immediately.

Ammo counter

Ammunition chamber

Barrel

Grip

The T-52 Carbine has a smart-linked optics system which is tethered to the hardware often worn by Covenant marksmen and snipers.

RADIOACTIVE ARSENAL

The Type-51 Carbine was designed by the Iruiru Armory on Sanghelios, based on marksman rifles used earlier in the Elites' war-dominated history. Its ammunition can come in a number of compositions, but the Covenant primarily employ an extremely toxic compound mined from a radioactive moon in the Elites' star system. The T-51 can fire this ballistic round (coated in shielded material) at 2,296 feet per second (700 m/s), which can effectively stop a target at up to 656 yards (600m). The Covenant Carbine is predominantly used by Elites and Jackal marksmen and is a lethal element of the Covenant's armament.

CUTTER
CAPTAIN JAMES GREGORY CUTTER

STATISTICS

HALO WARS

In Halo Wars, Captain Cutter supplies the player with orders and objectives while offering support from the UNSC *Spirit of Fire*.

FULL NAME: James Gregory Cutter
SERVICE NUMBER: 01730-58392-JC
BRANCH: UNSC Navy
GROUP: Third Fleet, Battle Group D
RANK: Captain
HEIGHT: 6ft 1in (185.4cm)
WEIGHT: 195lbs (88.5kg)
HOMEWORLD: Reach
DATE OF BIRTH: June 12, 2478

Captain James Cutter was handpicked by Admiral Preston Cole for the campaign above Harvest, where his resourcefulness and cunning proved unparalleled. He led his crew fearlessly, even in the face of death.

RECORD OF A VETERAN

Like many of the UNSC Navy's best, Cutter was well-learned in astrogation and command, having studied extensively at both the School of the North Star and the Officer Candidate School. On February 10, 2534, Cutter and the rest of the crew of the *Spirit of Fire* were declared "lost with all hands" by the UNSC, though their actual fate still remains a mystery.

Combat-ready uniform

Personal sidearm

EXPERIENCED OFFICER

There is no question about it: Captain Cutter is a true hero of the UNSC Navy. He had diligently served for decades before the Covenant arrived in 2525. After five excruciating years of tug of war for Harvest's survival, Cutter was sent by Admiral Preston to the frontlines aboard the UNSC *Spirit of Fire*. There, Cutter pursued the Covenant to Arcadia and on to the Forerunner shield world. He eventually defeated this Covenant contingent by initiating a stellar collapse, which unfortunately left his ship stranded.

CYCLOPS
HRUNTING MARK III [B] EXOSKELETON

Previous failures in the development of UNSC battle armor led a highly classified team to create "Cyclops," a one-man operated power suit with a nuclear energy supply, allowing for long periods of activity.

STATISTICS

HALO WARS

Cyclopes can be deployed during Halo Wars to repair UNSC equipment, while also capable of destroying the enemy's equipment with its powerful arms.

MANUFACTURER: Weapons Research (T12A)
DESIGNATION: HRUNTING Mark III [B] Exoskeleton
CREW: 1 operator
HEIGHT: 14.2ft (4.3m)
WIDTH: 11.7ft (3.6m)

Operator harness

Torque amplification gauntlets

PROJECT: HRUNTING/YGGDRASIL

Decades after the creation of the Cyclops, the same highly classified Algolis group would leverage this technology and ONI's MJOLNIR for an advanced prototype armor codenamed HRUNTING/YGGDRASIL.

Cyclopes were aboard the UNSC *Spirit of Fire* in 2531, assisting the crew when the ship engaged the Covenant on multiple worlds.

Hydraulic-buffered shocks

BREAKTHROUGH VARIANT

When the Mark III line of armored exoskeletons became defunct after its initial launch in 2510, the Office of Naval Intelligence (ONI) scrapped their plans for the armor, moving instead to Project: MJOLNIR. But in 2513, the UNSC research team from Algolis working on a separate military project known as HRUNTING evaluated the Mark III units, making their own breakthroughs which would result in the improved [B] variant, called "Cyclops." These machines were built for non-combat military roles, such as construction, transportation, terraforming, and traditional dock work. However, some have been fielded in combat situations, assisting with repairs, and in some rare instances, the destruction of enemy matériel and fortifications.

DARE

CAPTAIN VERONICA DARE

STATISTICS

HALO 3: ODST

Early on during the Halo 3: ODST campaign, the player seemingly witnesses the abduction of Dare at the hands of the Covenant. Only later is it discovered that she had not only eluded capture, but had succeeded in her high-priority mission.

FULL NAME: Veronica Dare
SERVICE NUMBER: [CLASSIFIED]
BRANCH: UNSC Navy
GROUP: Office of Naval Intelligence, Section One
RANK: Captain
HEIGHT: 5ft 7in (170cm)
WEIGHT: 153lbs (69.4kg)
HOMEWORLD: [CLASSIFIED]
DATE OF BIRTH: [CLASSIFIED]

Little is known about the ONI operative Veronica Dare, but her decisive role in the discovery of an ancient buried machine in 2552 led the UNSC to victory against the Covenant.

TIER ONE ASSET

Dare located a Covenant Engineer in the ONI data center which had downloaded vital information including the entity known as "Vergil," a subroutine of the city's AI.

Dare selected Edward Buck's ODST squad, despite a romantic fallout with him, as she knew the troopers would be reliable and well-trained.

ONI/ Recon PPE

S1-Recon BDU

S1/ONI Field Fatigues

DESPERATE MISSION

Like most agents of ONI, Captain Veronica Dare's role and purview within Section One was closely guarded. What is known is that on October 20, 2552, while the UNSC forces engaged the Covenant fleet above planet Earth, she requested a squad of ODSTs in an effort to procure crucial data from a secured location below New Mombasa's ONI Alpha Site. This data led humanity to a Forerunner machine buried near the town of Voi, which was capable of generating a Portal that could transport ships to the Ark installation. It was this enormous superstructure that in turn offered humanity a solution to end the war.

45

UNSC

DELTA HALO
INSTALLATION 05

Delta Halo was one of a number of ringworlds scattered across the galaxy by the Forerunners. Centuries before humanity located it, a containment breach led to a Flood outbreak and a Gravemind, putting the galaxy into peril.

Many of the structures littering the surface of Delta Halo strangely appear to be older than the ring itself.

Diameter: 6,214 miles (10,000km)

Surface width: 198 miles (318km)

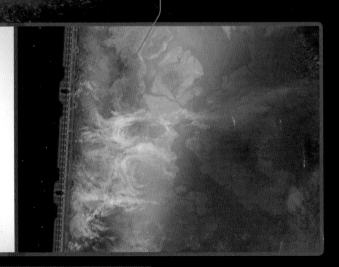

SITE OF A CIVIL WAR

Before firing the Halo Array, the Forerunners stored dormant specimens of the Flood on each installation for future study. They hoped to find a cure against the parasite in case it ever returned from beyond the galaxy's borders. However, when containment protocols on Delta Halo failed, the Flood threat re-emerged, this time from within the very thing intended to destroy it. On November 3, 2552, a Covenant civil war found its way to the surface of Delta Halo, and inadvertently gave the Flood passage off the installation to High Charity. On Delta Halo, fleets managed by the Elites began quarantining the installation, cauterizing its surface through orbital bombardment. Its current state remains a mystery.

DEPLOYABLE EQUIPMENT

DEPLOYABLE COMBAT MODIFICATION EQUIPMENT

STATISTICS

HALO 3

Halo 3 was the first Halo game to showcase deployable equipment.

TYPES/FORMS:
Active Camouflage
Auto Turret
Bubble Shield
Deployable Cover
Flare
Gravity Lift
Power Drain
Radar Jammer
Regenerator
Trip Mine

SHARED TECHNOLOGY:
As with weapons, humans and Covenant Brutes use all equipment retrieved from the battlefield regardless of origin. For example, humans regularly utilize power drain while the Brutes have no compunction against frequently deploying bubble shields.

During the war, both sides developed a number of deployable combat devices. While humanity's were essentially reverse-engineered Covenant machines, both had their roots in Forerunner technology.

Regenerator

Active cammo

Bubble shield

Power drain

Radar jammer

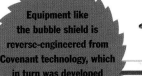

Deployable cover (closed)

Trip mine

Portable gravity lift

Deployable cover (open)

Equipment like the bubble shield is reverse-engineered from Covenant technology, which in turn was developed from Forerunner artifacts.

COMBAT MODIFICATION

The term "deployable equipment" is used to describe the gamut of apparatuses created by both the Covenant and the UNSC for use during the war. For the UNSC, the most notable were devices like the bubble shield (which creates a spherical protective energy field), the regenerator (which resets and regenerates shield tech), and the trip mine (which explodes when in close proximity to a target). For the Covenant, equipment like the flare (which briefly emits a blinding light), the portable gravity lift (an anti-gravity solution), the radar jammer (which scrambles motion tracking equipment), and the power drain (which drops nearby energy shields), were all important components of infantry combat.

DESTROYER
COVENANT SHIP CLASSIFICATION

The Covenant destroyer is a vessel intended specifically for pursuit and attack, although it can and has been used in lieu of cruisers and carriers for occupation needs.

STATISTICS

HALO WARS

Thus far, the only destroyers showcased in a Halo game have been the ones seen in Halo Wars.

CLASS: RPV (Light Destroyer)
LENGTH: 4,921ft (1,500m)
BEAM: 3,993ft (1,217m)
USE: Reconnaissance, pursuit

CLASS: CPV (Heavy Destroyer)
LENGTH: 5,459ft (1,664m)
BEAM: 4,429ft (1,350m)
USE: Assault, attack

PRIMARY ARMAMENT:
Ventral Cleansing Beam
SECONDARY ARMAMENT:
Anterior Plasma Cannon (2)
TERTIARY ARMAMENT:
Point Laser Defense

VESSELS OF DESTRUCTION

Destroyers within the Covenant naval fleets typically fall into one of two categories: RPV and CPV, though there are others serving in a lesser capacity. RPV-class vessels are usually sent in advance of an invasion and are used for escort on reconnaissance missions. They are smaller, but generally carry the same armament as CPV-class destroyers, which are designed to crush an opponent's resistance and initiate the Covenant's scorched earth policy of glassing their enemy's unfortunate worlds.

SIGMA OCTANUS IV

An RPV-class destroyer escorted two Covenant frigates and a carrier in a brief skirmish above Sigma Octanus IV. This battle preceded the larger conflict, which saw one of only a few human naval victories during the Covenant War.

During Admiral Cole's five-year campaign to retake Harvest, the Covenant used CPV-class destroyers in their effort to eliminate Harvest's human presence.

DMR
M392 DESIGNATED MARKSMAN RIFLE

STATISTICS

HALO: REACH

Fictionally, the DMR has a number of firing modes, however, its semi-automatic mode is the one used throughout Halo: Reach.

MANUFACTURER: Misriah Armory
DESIGNATION: M392 Designated Marksman Rifle
AMMUNITION: 7.62 x 51mm FMJ-AP
MAGAZINE CAPACITY: 15 rounds
LENGTH: 42.9in (109cm)
FIRING MODE: Automatic, semi-automatic

The DMR is an air-cooled, gas-operated rifle designed for mid to long-range combat. While other UNSC branches have moved to the Battle Rifle, the M392 is still favored by the Army.

Thanks to their reliability in the field, ballistic weapons like the M392 have gone largely unchanged for centuries.

EVOS-D scope

Pistol grip

Fire select mode

BULLPUP DESIGN

The M392, like many rifles the UNSC fields in the 26th century, has a familiar bullpup design, where the weapon's reloading action occurs behind the trigger.

PRECISION WEAPON

The M392 Designated Marksman Rifle is an extraordinary weapon capable of firing at range with incredible accuracy. The DMR saw widespread use throughout the UNSC during the Insurrection and for a large portion of the Covenant War, but its use decreased with the rise in popularity of the BR55HB Service Rifle in 2548. Recognizing the DMR's reliability and efficacy on the battlefield, the UNSC Army was reluctant to withdraw its use of the rifle, and continued to field it all the way into late 2552, including at the Battle for Reach.

DREADNOUGHT
FORERUNNER SHIP CLASSIFICATION

The ancient Dreadnought is a vessel engineered by the Forerunners to access their gateway portals buried on worlds throughout the galaxy. These portals offer passage to the Forerunners' Ark installation.

BEFORE THE COVENANT

Long before the formation of the Covenant, the Prophets found the abandoned Dreadnought on their homeworld. They later used it to leave their planet in search of other Forerunner relics, and soon encountered the Elites. In a battle for supremacy between the two races, the Dreadnought helped the Prophets prevail. They forced the Elites into a treaty that led to the rise of the Covenant.

After the war with the Elites, the Prophets decommissioned the Dreadnought as a show of peace.

Strut

Construct armature

Prow

PATH TO THE ARK

For many years the Forerunner Dreadnought lay at the heart of the Covenant's Holy City of High Charity, providing power and a central point of worship for their mobile homeworld. But when the High Prophet of Truth discovered the location of a Portal on Earth which would lead to the Ark, he abandoned High Charity, taking the Dreadnought with him to lead a vast Covenant fleet to Earth. There, the vessel landed atop an ancient machine which generated the Portal, propelling Truth and his forces to the Ark. Unfortunately for the Covenant, the Ark and the Dreadnought were both subsequently destroyed by the Master Chief.

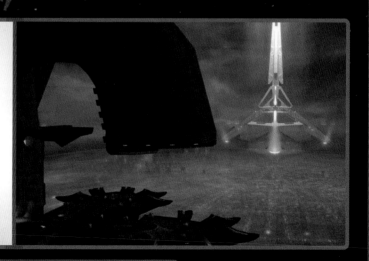

DRONES
YANME'E

Drones are quite intelligent, but their anatomy makes communication with other Covenant species difficult.

Intelligent arthropods from the planet Palamok, Drones were initially integrated into the Covenant as workers, but later they became a formidable fighting force within the alliance's infantry.

STRENGTH IN NUMBERS

As the name "Drones" suggests, these hive-creatures follow orders dispassionately and unquestioningly. They accept the hierarchal power structure of the Covenant as it is reminiscent of the systems on Palamok. Centuries ago, when the Covenant first arrived on Palamok, the ensuing conflict was devastating for both sides, but the Drones eventually relented and accepted their civilization's assimilation into the collective. For a long time they served in a largely custodial capacity, working in areas of maintenance and repair, but they were later integrated into the Covenant's military structure. Though they are not particularly strong or well-suited for combat individually, in large numbers they form a very real threat and can overwhelm enemies from airborne positions.

STATISTICS

HALO 2 • HALO 3 • HALO 3: ODST • HALO: REACH

Drones first appeared in the Halo 2 mission "Cairo Station."

SPECIES: Yanme'e, *Turpis rex*
AVERAGE HEIGHT: 5ft 10in to 6ft 9in (177.8cm to 205.8cm)
AVERAGE WEIGHT: 169.7lbs to 279.9lbs (77kg to 127kg)
HOMEWORLD: Palamok
TYPES/FORMS: Unmutual, Minor, Major, Leader, Queen

Tactile hands

Tough exoskeleton

ASSISTED FLIGHT

Drones fly quite well in 1.0 G environments. This is largely due to their evolutionary lineage on the heavy 2.0 G world of Palamok and the gravity dampening modules they have affixed to their bodies.

Chitinous membrane

DROP POD
SINGLE-OCCUPANT EXOATMOSPHERIC INSERTION VEHICLE

The drop pod is used as a means of troop deployment from very high altitudes or, in most cases, from space. This equipment is most frequently employed by Orbital Drop Shock Troopers (ODST).

STATISTICS

HALO 2 • HALO 3 • HALO WARS • HALO 3: ODST

In Halo 3: ODST's opening Campaign mission, players get to experience a drop within an SOEIV while being deployed to New Mombasa from the UNSC cruiser *Say My Name.*

MANUFACTURER: Ushuaia Armory
DESIGNATION: Single-Occupant Exoatmospheric Insertion Vehicle
CREW: 1 operator
HEIGHT: 16.4ft (5m)
LENGTH: 7.7ft (2.3m)
WIDTH: 8.7ft (2.7m)

Braking chute system

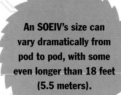

An SOEIV's size can vary dramatically from pod to pod, with some even longer than 18 feet (5.5 meters).

ORBITAL DEPLOYMENT

The Single-Occupant Exoatmospheric Insertion Vehicle (SOEIV), commonly referred to as a drop pod, is a class of Human Entry Vehicle (HEV). Within a standard SOEIV is a crash seat with secured belts, controls for maneuvering the pod, and communication systems which allow synchronization with others during deployment. Once a successful drop has been achieved, the hatch is expelled by way of an explosive gas-bolt system triggered by the occupant. While this sort of deployment has been refined over time, many drops can still end unsuccessfully due to equipment malfunction or user error.

SAFETY IN NUMBERS

Despite the obvious danger inherent with SOEIV deployment, these drops have a lower overall attrition rate in combat than conventional dropship deployment. This is largely due to the fact that each soldier is being conveyed separately instead of together in one craft.

Reinforced impact plating

DUTCH
CORPORAL TAYLOR H. MILES

Dutch primarily operates as a Heavy Weapons Specialist and his battle dress uniform (BDU) has been customized for this role.

The extensive military career of Corporal Taylor H. Miles, or "Dutch," encompassed several campaigns before he found himself fighting on the streets of New Mombasa, at humanity's darkest hour.

STATISTICS

HALO 3: ODST

Players can step into Dutch's shoes in Halo 3: ODST's mission "Uplift Reserve," where the ODST must trek across a Covenant-occupied nature reserve in New Mombasa.

FULL NAME: Taylor H. Miles
SERVICE NUMBER: 21175-12121-TM
BRANCH: UNSC Marine Corps
GROUP: Naval Special Weapons, Orbital Drop Shock Troopers
RANK: Corporal
HEIGHT: 6ft 3in (190cm)
WEIGHT: 200lbs (91kg)
HOMEWORLD: Mars
DATE OF BIRTH: June 3, 2519

M/LBE Hard Case

ODST-HS Combat Helmet

M6C/SOCOM

PAINFUL REMINDER

Dutch's wife, Gretchen, was removed from combat when she lost her leg to a rebel mine. This event weighed heavily on him throughout the remainder of his career.

HEAVY WEAPONS SPECIALIST

Born on Mars in 2519, Taylor Miles began a career as a road train driver before joining the UNSC Marine Corps and later moving to the Orbital Drop Shock Troopers. It was there that he befriended Kojo "Romeo" Agu and his future wife, Gretchen Ketola. On October 20, 2552, he was deployed in New Mombasa, fighting against the Covenant who had arrived only hours earlier. After tracking the enemy to a local Office of Naval Intelligence site, Dutch and his squad managed to secure important data that revealed the Covenant's true intentions on Earth: to locate an artifact that would lead them to the Ark.

EARTH
SOL III

As the cradle world of the human race since its earliest beginnings, and the final battleground in the war against the Covenant, no planet holds as much significance to humanity as Earth.

Earth once had six space elevators, but during the Covenant's occupation, New Mombasa and Havana's were destroyed.

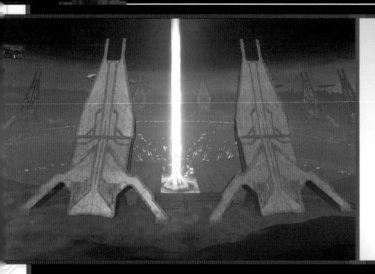

FORERUNNER LEGACY

Roughly one hundred millennia ago, Earth, being a classic 1-G/1-atm world favorable for evolutionary stability, was the site of the Forerunner event known as the Conservation Measure. This incident involved the Forerunners burying an enormous machine below Earth's surface, which could create a Portal leading directly to the their Ark installation, far beyond the galactic rim. After discovering the machine and the legacy it held, humanity used the Ark as the final battleground against the Covenant and as a way to end the looming threat of the Flood, unleashed on Delta Halo only weeks earlier.

STATISTICS

HALO 2 • HALO 3 • HALO 3: ODST

In the Halo 2 mission "Cairo Station," players can see humanity's homeworld in the skybox.

STAR, POSITION: Sol, III
SATELLITE(S): Luna
GRAVITY: 1.0 G
ATMOSPHERE: 1 atm (N_2, O_2, Ar)
SURFACE TEMPERATURE: −4°F to 104°F (−20°C to 40°C)
MAJOR CITIES: Cairo, Chicago, London, New Mombasa, Quito, Sydney
POPULATION: 200,000,000 (post-war)
SPACE TETHERS: 6 (pre-war); 4 (post-war)

Diameter: 7,926 miles (12,756km)

AN ANCIENT WAR

Earth was in danger of overpopulation in the late 21st century, until the human race began colonizing the Sol system. Hundreds of years later, at the close of the Covenant War, its population had been reduced to roughly 200 million.

ELEPHANT
M313 HEAVY RECOVERY VEHICLE

STATISTICS

HALO 3 • HALO WARS • HALO 3: ODST

In Halo 3: ODST, the Olifant was an Elephant-variant used as a commercial garbage truck.

MANUFACTURER: JOTUN Heavy Industries
DESIGNATION: M313 Heavy Recovery Vehicle
CREW: 1 driver + 12 to 16 crew
LENGTH: 84.3ft (25.7m)
WIDTH: 44.5ft (13.6m)
PRIMARY ARMAMENT: M41 Light Anti-Aircraft Gun

The Elephant is one of the largest ground vehicles the UNSC has at its disposal. It is used primarily as a mobile recovery platform for withdrawing high-value equipment from behind enemy lines.

M41 LAAG

Operator station

Elephants are designed to safely transport troops, equipment, and light vehicles to and from the frontlines of a conflict.

Crane system

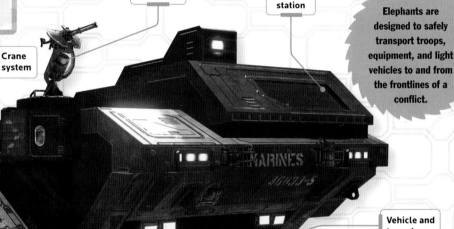

Vehicle and troop bay

M312 ELEPHANT

The M312 HRV is an Elephant variant with a protected rear bay, additional weapon emplacements, and the capacity to deploy personnel in hostile territory.

RETRIEVAL AND RECOVERY

Designed by Mars-based JOTUN Heavy Industries, HRVs originally found a foothold in both the utility and farming industries during the early years of colonial expansion. After decades of exemplary performance, the UNSC contracted JOTUN to build what they referred to as Mobile Assault, Support, and Recovery Platforms, or "Elephants." The M312, M313, and M318 HRV variants are the most commonly seen across various theatres of war, all bearing unique functional designs which favor specific operations and combat scenarios.

ELITE ASCETIC
COVENANT MINISTRY OF ABNEGATION/ASCETICS

Fueled by their zeal for Covenant doctrine, the Ascetic Elites represent and defend ideological purity. While their kind was dormant for many centuries, their class was resurrected during the Great Schism.

STATISTICS

HALO 3

Ascetic armor appears exclusively in Halo 3 and is one of many Elite armor variants available in multiplayer.

SPECIES: Sangheili
MINISTRY: Ministry of Abnegation
GROUP: Ascetics
LOCATION: High Charity
FUNCTION: Ideological control/ enforcement, exegetics, applied hermeneutics, philology

Ancient helmet design

Ascetic combat harness

The Elite Ascetic helmet maintains the traditional and threatening bladed mandible-guard.

ADVANCING THEIR FAITH

Prior to the formation of the Covenant, the Ascetics were a sect of fervent Elites who defended the purity of their faith. One of the terms of the Writ of Union, however, was the dissolution and reconstitution of the Ascetic guard under the Prophets' newly formed Ministry of Abnegation. For centuries this was the case, until the events of the Great Schism, when the Elite Ascetics were resurrected to fight against the traitorous Prophets and the Brutes who served them.

STATISTICS

HALO: REACH

In Halo: Reach, Elite Generals fill the familiar role of Brute Chieftains, though the game features both impressive enemies.

SPECIES: Sangheili
GROUP: Field Command of Occupational Forces
LOCATION: Disputed groundside territories
FUNCTION: Command of groundside units, troop deployment, strategic execution
ARMAMENT: Energy Sword, Plasma Launcher, Fuel Rod Gun, Concussion Rifle, Needle Rifle

Elite Generals are one of the highest-ranking military personnel employed by the Covenant among their groundside forces. They can both command and personally lead troops into battle.

Command helmet

FIELD COMMAND

Elite Generals command troops of hundreds or even thousands, managing ground operations when the direct occupation of an enemy's territory is necessary. During some campaigns, multiple generals are required, each working in concert with each other to handle individual insurgencies and conflicts wherever they crop up. While they specialize in command, Elite Generals are particularly lethal in combat. Their armor is heavily augmented and their weapons are formidable.

CHAIN OF COMMAND

Depending on the nature of a given military operation, generals can report directly to a field marshal or even a fleet's supreme commander.

Enhanced shielding

Elite Generals were present on Reach, coordinating their military efforts first across the Viery territory and then the entire planet.

ELITE RANGER
COVENANT SPECIAL WARFARE GROUP/FLEET SECURITY

One of the Covenant military's many specialized units, the Elite Rangers are a class of highly skilled Fleet Security soldiers which focuses largely on extra-vehicular space combat.

The armor used by Elite Rangers has been upgraded to allow for combat in exotic environments that lack oxygen.

VERSATILE FIGHTING FORCE

The Elite Rangers are clad in armor that can not only protect them against the extremes of space, but provides them with full mobility when fighting enemy infantry in zero or low-gravity conditions, without the aid of traditional vessels. Their flight equipment can also be fielded planetside, particularly when the Covenant require an extremely mobile infantry force, an advance scouting detachment, or even simply an augmentation of existing combat teams. Whatever their use, Elite Rangers are highly valued and extremely proficient at their role.

EVA faceshield

HONED FOR SPACE

Elite Rangers fight in most theaters of war. However, they specialize in zero-gravity conditions and for this reason they are used sparingly in ground engagements.

STATISTICS

HALO 2 • HALO: REACH

Elite Rangers were first encountered in Halo 2's mission "Cairo Station," where they attempted to hamper the Master Chief's efforts against the Covenant boarding parties.

SPECIES: Sangheili
GROUP: Special Warfare Group, Fleet Security
LOCATION: Nearly all fields of combat
FUNCTION: Extra-vehicular activity, unconventional warfare, specialized reconnaissance
ARMAMENT: Plasma Rifle, Plasma Repeater, Needle Rifle, Focus Rifle

Assault harness

Corvette landing platform

STATISTICS

**HALO: COMBAT EVOLVED • HALO 2
HALO 3 • HALO: REACH**

In Halo 2, the player, as the Arbiter, leads a strike force, fighting alongside the esteemed SpecOps commander Rtas 'Vadumee.

SPECIES: Sangheili
GROUP: Special Warfare Group/ Special Operations
LOCATION: Nearly all fields of combat
FUNCTION: Special operations, unconventional warfare, infiltration
ARMAMENT: Energy Sword, Plasma Rifle, Needle Rifle

Special Operations (SpecOps) is the Covenant Special Warfare Group's division for unconventional warfare. The goal of these Elite-commanded soldiers is to subvert and discretely hinder the enemy.

Despite the lack of overlap among Covenant military groups, Special Operations works closely with Fleet and Home Security.

COVERT MISSIONS

Elites within Special Operations execute classified missions, typically working in concert with conventional warfare groups to infiltrate enemy fortifications and provide advance reconnaissance, or even to initiate guerilla warfare where necessary. During the Covenant War, commanding officers regularly used SpecOps strike teams to hunt down specific targets, to penetrate enemy lines, and to provide advance scouting intel. Despite their success against the UNSC, a SpecOps Commander named Rtas 'Vadumee led a fleet of renegade Elites back to Earth and with the help of the Arbiter, forged a tentative agreement with the humans that resulted in the destruction of the Covenant.

Infiltration harness

BEYOND ELITES

While other Covenant species may operate within the SpecOps group, they are never in command and are always under the close supervision of their Elite handlers.

Embedded camo tech

As their name indicates, Zealots are by far the most passionate of their kind. They are resilient, powerful, and entirely devoted to the pursuit of finding Forerunner artifacts to further their faith.

Advanced shielding tech

Improved combat helmet

STATISTICS

HALO: COMBAT EVOLVED • HALO 2
HALO: REACH

The extremely skilled Zealots have proved to be some of the most challenging enemies in Halo games. Their gold-armored iterations in Halo: Combat Evolved wielded energy swords with ruthless efficiency.

SPECIES: Sangheili
MINISTRY: Ministry of Fervent Intercession
GROUP: Zealots
LOCATION: Reliquary frontlines
FUNCTION: Apostolic delivery and coercion, reliquary acquisition
ARMAMENT:
Energy Sword, Plasma Rifle, Needle Rifle, Concussion Rifle

T-50 Concussion Rifle

TARGETING VISEGRÁD
Zealot Elites were responsible for the death of Professor Laszlo Sorvad, an operation that led them to several Forerunner relics scattered across Reach.

UNQUESTIONED LOYALTY

The name "Zealot" represents a category of high-ranking Elites that forms the razor's edge of any significant Covenant military operation. Unparalleled in skill, these cunning squads are used by the Ministry of Fervent Intercession to locate, analyze, and amass intel regarding reliquary sites, the physical aggregation of Forerunner artifacts and technology in one location. This can be done several ways, but is usually resolved through apostolic intervention by force or, in the case of humanity, through the eradication of a heretical species.

STATISTICS

HALO: COMBAT EVOLVED
HALO 2 • HALO 3 • HALO WARS
HALO 3: ODST • HALO: REACH

Elites have long since been regarded as the most challenging and gratifying enemy to defeat in Halo.

SPECIES: Sangheili, *Macto cognatus*
AVERAGE HEIGHT: 7ft 4in to 8ft 6in (223cm to 259cm)
AVERAGE WEIGHT: 307lbs to 393lbs (139kg to 178kg)
HOMEWORLD: Sanghelios
TYPES/FORMS:
Minor, Major, Ultra, Ranger, Special Operations, Zealot, General, Field Marshall, Shipmaster, Supreme Commander, Imperial Commander, Honor Guard, Councilor

The Elites are a saurian species from the planet Sanghelios. Their conflict with the Prophets resulted in the formation of the Covenant, and the Elites taking control of its military ventures.

Pronounced mandibles

Saurian bipedal posture

The Elite culture is a feudalistic patriarchal society that focuses on war, honor, and the honing of combat skills

BRED FOR WAR

Before war with the humans, the Elites fought against the Prophets over the appropriate use of Forerunner artifacts, but this conflict eventually resulted in a truce. After the Covenant stumbled upon humanity, a violent campaign against the species ensued, bringing it to the brink of extinction. Only in the final days of war did some Elites begin to doubt the Prophets. This schism led to a civil war that resulted in the Elites aligning with their human foes to prevent the High Prophet of Truth from firing Halo.

EMILE
WARRANT OFFICER EMILE-A239, SPARTAN-III

Though unruly and oftentimes overzealous, SPARTAN-III Emile-A239 was fiercely dedicated to the UNSC, particularly to his comrades on Noble Team. He proved indispensable against the Covenant's war machine at Reach.

STATISTICS

HALO: REACH

In the Halo: Reach mission "Pillar of Autumn," the player is accompanied by Emile as they make their final run to the *Autumn* to deliver Cortana.

FULL NAME: Emile-A239
SERVICE NUMBER: S-A239
BRANCH: UNSC Army
GROUP: Special Warfare, Group Three
RANK: Warrant Officer
HEIGHT: 6ft 10in (208.4cm)
WEIGHT: 234.7lbs (106.5kg)
HOMEWORLD: Eridanus II
DATE OF BIRTH: March 11, 2523
DATE OF DEATH: August 30, 2552

Mk. V—EVA [C]

Emile was born in Luxor on the colonial world of Eridanus II, a rebel stronghold until the Covenant razed it in 2530.

Kukri knife

M45 Shotgun

UNCHECKED AUDACITY

On occasion, Emile has clashed with his commanders over his use of force, particularly against rebels.

PRESENT UNTIL THE END

After years of training and augmentation, the orphan known as Emile became a SPARTAN-III super-soldier for Alpha Company, fighting the Covenant across human-occupied space. He later found himself on Noble Team, an elite strike force within the Special Warfare division. During the Fall of Reach, Emile-A239 and fellow Spartan Noble Six were entrusted with the safe delivery of Cortana to the *Pillar of Autumn*. They succeeded in their mission, but Emile sacrificed his life in the process. Like the other members of Noble, he will be remembered as a hero who bravely fought and died in defense of the planet Reach.

ENERGY SWORD
TYPE-1 ENERGY WEAPON/SWORD

THE MASTER CHIEF

In the wake of the Battle of Miridem in 2544, the Master Chief engaged the Elite Thel 'Lodamee in a brief but intense battle with Energy Swords.

The Energy Sword is easily the most lethal close-quarters weapon within the Covenant arsenal. Its twin razor-sharp blades are formed from superheated plasma and can easily cleave a human in two.

Shaped Plasma

Hilt

Field generator

Outside of the Covenant military, only Elite aristocrats are allowed to wield swords.

STATISTICS

HALO: COMBAT EVOLVED • HALO 2
HALO 3 • HALO WARS • HALO: REACH

The Energy Sword is a much sought after weapon in Halo multiplayer as it allows players to lunge toward their enemy for a swift kill.

MANUFACTURER: Merchants of Qikost
DESIGNATION: Type-1 Energy Weapon/Sword
AMMUNITION: Shaped Plasma
ENERGY CAPACITY: 100 units
LENGTH: 49.9in
(126.8cm)

TRADITIONAL WEAPONRY

Following the Elites' longstanding tradition of swords and bladed weapons, the Type-1 Energy Weapon/Sword, generally known as the Energy Sword, was designed to execute lethal strikes in the hands of a well-trained combatant. Historically seen as a noble weapon, the Energy Sword is aligned with the Elites' rigid sense of honor. Demanding the utmost skill and precision from its user, the sword is carried by high-ranking Elites such as Zealots, SpecOps, and Generals.

ENGINEERS
HURAGOK

Unlike other species in the Covenant, Engineers are not organic, but a composition of nanomechanical substances that look and function like organic material. They repair existing technology, amongst other functions.

STATISTICS

HALO WARS • HALO: 3 ODST
HALO: REACH

In Halo games, Engineers typically provide their nearby allies with health or additional shielding.

SPECIES: Huragok, *Facticius indoles*
HEIGHT: 5ft 11in to 8ft 2in (180cm to 248cm)
AVERAGE WEIGHT: 123lbs (56kg)

Gas sacks

Reproduction occurs between two to three Huragok and takes under an hour with enough raw materials; the more participants, the quicker the process.

FORCED SERVITUDE

When the Brute-led Covenant forces occupied New Mombasa, they used explosive harnesses to both control Engineers and booby trap them against anyone curious enough to engage these naturally docile and cooperative creatures.

Tentacles

MYSTERIOUS SAVANTS

Huragok, or Engineers, were collected from M-series Forerunner facilities by the Prophets prior to the establishment of the Covenant. They have been used ever since in the repair, reconstitution, and augmentation of various technologies, primarily those belonging to the Covenant themselves. Though this is their main function, they have others, including the exploration of Forerunner artifacts and the secured transmission of data from one location to another. Engineers have been present throughout all of the Covenant War, though they were rarely witnessed by the UNSC until late in the conflict.

A WEIGHTY ISSUE

Engineers are named by their parents according to their initial buoyancy when the reproduction process is complete. This results in names such as *Lighter Than Some*, *Easy To Adjust*, and *Far Too Heavy*.

Multiple eyes

EOD ARMOR

STATISTICS

HALO 3 • HALO: REACH

In Halo: Reach's Armory, players must acquire the rank of Sergeant and spend 15,000 credits before gaining access to the EOD armor variant.

SERIES: Mark V/Mark VI
MANUFACTURER: Materials Group
TESTING SITE: Damascus Materials Testing Facility

Explosive Ordnance Disposal (EOD) armor was engineered for improved survivability near an explosion, following a dramatic naval skirmish between the UNSC and the Covenant near Chi Ceti IV.

Mk. V—EOD/CNM

SUPERIOR PROTECTION

When the first Spartan was killed in action just outside their front door, the Materials Group located in Chi Ceti IV began an internal study on how to improve survivability near an explosion. For years, the intel gleaned from this was discretely integrated into MJOLNIR's technology platform, continuing to support Mark IV's various iterations. But when Mark V went into production, the Materials Group had already fashioned a specific variant known as EOD, providing increased protection against explosions in the user's immediate vicinity.

EOD uses an advanced pressure dispersal system, though as a result, the armor loses key interface components due to space constraints.

PAVING THE WAY

EOD was fielded by Spartans deep behind enemy lines, allowing them to navigate dangerous territory and neutralize mine fields before imminent UNSC incursions.

UA/CA plate

Mk. V—Ceramic composition

EVA ARMOR
MJOLNIR POWERED ASSAULT ARMOR/V—EXTRA VEHICULAR ACTIVITY (EVA)

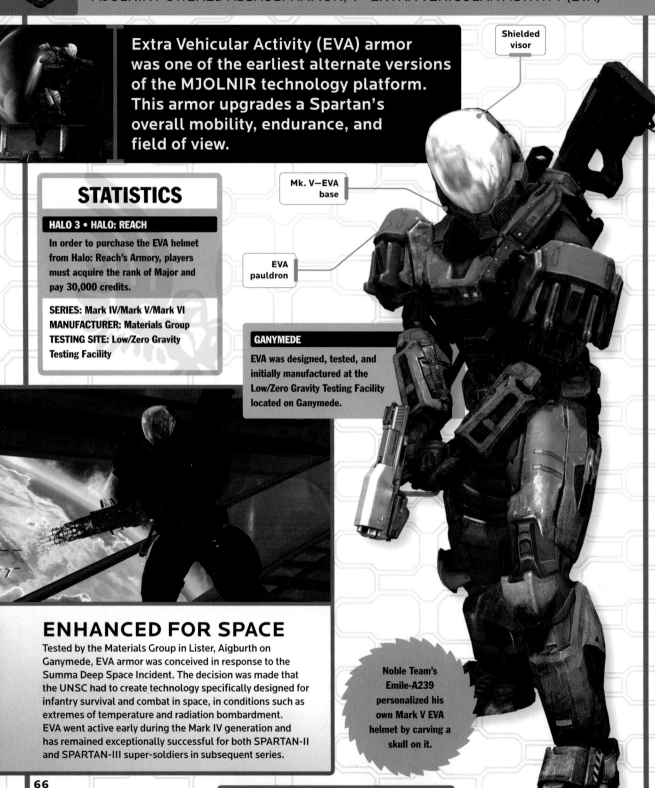

Extra Vehicular Activity (EVA) armor was one of the earliest alternate versions of the MJOLNIR technology platform. This armor upgrades a Spartan's overall mobility, endurance, and field of view.

Shielded visor

Mk. V—EVA base

EVA pauldron

STATISTICS

HALO 3 • HALO: REACH

In order to purchase the EVA helmet from Halo: Reach's Armory, players must acquire the rank of Major and pay 30,000 credits.

SERIES: Mark IV/Mark V/Mark VI
MANUFACTURER: Materials Group
TESTING SITE: Low/Zero Gravity Testing Facility

GANYMEDE

EVA was designed, tested, and initially manufactured at the Low/Zero Gravity Testing Facility located on Ganymede.

ENHANCED FOR SPACE

Tested by the Materials Group in Lister, Aigburth on Ganymede, EVA armor was conceived in response to the Summa Deep Space Incident. The decision was made that the UNSC had to create technology specifically designed for infantry survival and combat in space, in conditions such as extremes of temperature and radiation bombardment. EVA went active early during the Mark IV generation and has remained exceptionally successful for both SPARTAN-II and SPARTAN-III super-soldiers in subsequent series.

Noble Team's Emile-A239 personalized his own Mark V EVA helmet by carving a skull on it.

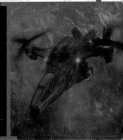

STATISTICS

HALO: REACH

Halo: Reach players can find the UH-144A only in Campaign, while the UH-144S appears in both Campaign and multiplayer.

The Falcon is the UNSC's primary utility helicopter in a sizeable fleet of VTOL crafts. The two most common Falcons are the "Attack" (UH-144A) and "Support" (UH-144S) variants, differing only in their armament.

MANUFACTURER:
Misriah Armory
DESIGNATION: Utility Helicopter-144
CREW: 1 pilot + 5 passengers
(including 2 door gunners)
LENGTH: 37.5ft (11.4m)
WIDTH: 32.8ft (10m)
PRIMARY ARMAMENT:
M638 20mm Autocannon
SECONDARY ARMAMENT:
Attack/M460 40mm Automatic
Grenade Launcher (2)
TERTIARY ARMAMENT:
Support/M247H 12.7mm Heavy
Machine Gun (2)

Cockpit

M638
Autocannon

Passenger/
crew bay

EFFECTIVE TRANSPORT

The UH-144 Falcon's open cabin, its heavy weaponry, and its impressive maneuverability make it ideal for the tight confines of many battlefields, whether that be a narrow canyon or a skyscraper-heavy metropolis. The pilot resides in an enclosed cockpit, while crewmembers have the choice of two gunner seats in extended buckets, two interior passenger seats, an aft bench, or any available standing room. With a chin-mounted 20mm autocannon and a pair of modular door guns, the Falcon's arsenal is unquestionably effective.

FLAME GRENADE
TYPE-3 ANTIPERSONNEL/ANTI-MATÉRIEL INCENDIARY GRENADE

This explosive device is a vicious implement devised by Brutes and frequently used against both equipment and humans with predictably horrific results. It uses a hazardous chemical compound containing Caesium.

SACRED PROMISSORY

The Sacred Promissory was the sole manufacturer of the Brute's T-3 AP/AM Incendiary Grenade just a few months prior to the Great Schism. This group's name sprouted from early contract negotiations between the Elites and the Prophets for the fabrication and production of weapons with improved technology. By the end of the war, and upon secret orders from the Prophet of Truth, the Sacred Promissory focused entirely on heavily arming the Covenant's Brute contingent.

Standard flame grenades only burn for five seconds, though Brutes have employed versions with longer burn cycles.

Caesium mixture

Steel casing

BRUTE FIREBOMB

While exploring the geological composition of their harsh homeworld Doisac, the Brutes developed a hazardous yet stable chemical compound using the pyrophoric alkali metal Caesium. When this mixture meets oxygen, it quickly ignites and burns at 3992°F (2200°C). Ironically for the Brutes, using these grenades prevents another favored type of barbarity: The Caesium mixture is a toxic substance and so Brutes cannot consume any human flesh after it has made contact with the reactive liquid.

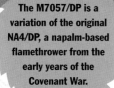

The M7057/DP is a variation of the original NA4/DP, a napalm-based flamethrower from the early years of the Covenant War.

The M7057/DP is a conventional, chemical-based flamethrower, which directs and ignites a stream of Pyrosene-V at up to a range of 44 feet (13.4m) with an undeniable psychological effect in combat.

Pyrosene-V tank

Fore grip

PSYCH CONCERNS

Soldiers who have used flamethrowers in combat are automatically earmarked for extensive psychological evaluation.

Heat shroud

STATISTICS

HALO 3 • HALO WARS

In Halo 3, the Flamethrower is an incredibly effective tool to use against the Flood parasite.

MANUFACTURER: Misriah Armory
DESIGNATION: M7057/Defoliant Projector
AMMUNITION: Pyrosene-V
MAGAZINE CAPACITY: 9 x three-second bursts
LENGTH: 66in (167.6cm)
FIRING MODE: Semi-automatic

BRINGING HELL

The defoliant projector was made specifically for the removal of brush and foliage in-theater or to establish a base. Though uncommon, there have been stories of soldiers using the M7057/DP in combat situations, specifically during the UNSC's campaign against the Covenant. Toward the end of the war, encounters with the Flood parasite led to the effective use of both this flamethrower and its older brother, the NA4/DP, which is often carried by the specialized marines codenamed "Hellbringers."

FLOOD
LF.XX.3273

The Flood is a virulent, parasitic species discovered approximately 100,000 years ago by the Forerunners. It was destroyed by the activation of Halo, but the parasite once again reared its collective head in the 26th century.

STATISTICS

HALO: COMBAT EVOLVED
HALO 2 • HALO 3 • HALO WARS

SPECIES: LF.Xx.3273 [FSC],
Inferi redivivus
TYPES/FORMS:
Infection Form, Combat Form,
Carrier Form, Stalker Form,
Ranged Form, Tank Form

PURITY IN TIME

The Flood's growth begins with the Feral Stage, where it requires organic hosts to propagate. Next comes the Coordinated Stage, when it can produce "pure" offspring such as the Tank Form.

"Pure" Tank Form

FSC-formed appendage

Some Flood can be dispatched by targeting the latent Infection Form, typically buried deep within their torso or head.

Infection forms

INSIDIOUS PARASITE

Lifeform.Xx.3273 FSC (Flood Super Cell) is the base component of the extragalactic parasite known as the Flood, a species which thrives on the consumption of sentient life. In an effort to prevent the parasite's spread, the Forerunners were forced to destroy all sentient life in the galaxy. Centuries later, humanity came into contact with Flood specimens on the Halo rings, resulting in yet another potentially cataclysmic outbreak. The Flood met its end a second time when the parasite's collective embodiment, an entity known as a Gravemind, reached the Ark, where it was destroyed when the Master Chief fired a nearby Halo installation.

STATISTICS

HALO: REACH

Continued fire with the Focus Rifle will quickly strip an enemy of both their shields and their health.

MANUFACTURER: Assembly Forges
DESIGNATION: Type-52 Special Applications Rifle
AMMUNITION: Electromagnetically Guided Plasma
ENERGY CAPACITY: 100 units
LENGTH: 57.2in (145.2cm)
FIRING MODE: Automatic

As with much Covenant weaponry, the Focus Rifle is based on reverse-engineered Forerunner technology. It utilizes superheated plasma energy focused in a single constant beam.

The Focus Rifle's coil set, like that on other Covenant weapons, is the cylindrical module where the plasma is formed.

Optics system

Coil set

Accelerator firing channel

ASSEMBLY FORGES

While the T-52 Focus Rifle is quite different from the T-50 Particle Beam Rifle in performance, both were developed by the same group within High Charity's Assembly Forges.

SPECIALIZED RIFLE

The Focus Rifle works much like the weapons mounted on Sentinels. While the exact nature of such Forerunner weapons remains a mystery, the Covenant attempted, with some success, to replicate that technology. The Focus Rifle utilizes electromagnetic coils to force the plasma down an extremely precise accelerator channel. The rifle requires a heavy power expenditure, easily depleting the battery; thus, the weapon must be used sparingly and judiciously. For this reason, it was primarily intended for marksmen and it functions in the same capacity as a sniper rifle.

FORGE
SERGEANT JOHN FORGE

Although often unruly, Sergeant John Forge proved to be one of the UNSC's finest soldiers, having fearlessly led the marines aboard the *Spirit of Fire* in their fight against the Covenant.

Forge's insubordination once had him serve time in prison, hampering any possibility of promotion.

STATISTICS

HALO WARS

In Halo Wars, Sergeant Forge's hero and leader abilities revolve around powerful ground-based vehicles like the Gauss Hog and Grizzly tank.

FULL NAME: John Forge
SERVICE NUMBER: 63492-94758-JF
BRANCH: UNSC Marine Corps
GROUP: Thirteenth Battalion, Foxtrot Company
RANK: Sergeant
HEIGHT: 6ft 3in (190.5cm)
WEIGHT: 215lbs (97.5kg)
HOMEWORLD: Earth
DATE OF BIRTH: May 29, 2501
DATE OF DEATH: February 25, 2531

TRUE CUNNING

Though physically outmatched, Forge managed to defeat the legendary Arbiter Ripa 'Moramee, when the Elite began gloating over what should have been an easy kill.

Battle pauldron

M6C Magnum

HEROIC SACRIFICE

John Forge frequently found himself in trouble thanks to his various acts of insubordination and conduct unbecoming an officer. Nevertheless, this sergeant's dedication to the Corps remained unquestionable, as witnessed during Admiral Cole's campaign on Harvest. Not only did Forge personally secure the crew of the UNSC *Prophecy*, but aboard the *Spirit of Fire*, he provided field leadership during a number of conflicts on Harvest, Arcadia, and the Forerunner shield world. It was there, on that artificial planet, that Forge sacrificed his own life to buy the UNSC *Spirit of Fire* enough time to escape.

FORKLIFT
S-2 TRAXUS CARGO TRANSPORTER

Although not technically a UNSC-commissioned vehicle, the S-2 Traxus Cargo Transporter, or forklift, is utilized across a number of key military sites. Its role is extraordinarily simple: to lift things.

EXTENUATING CIRCUMSTANCES

Plans for an S-3 forklift were well underway at a Traxus site in Voi, Kenya, but they were taken offline on November 17, 2552, due to "extenuating circumstances"—the Covenant's second invasion.

STATISTICS

HALO 3 • HALO 3: ODST • HALO: REACH

Halo: Reach allowed players to drive the forklift for the very first time.

MANUFACTURER: Traxus Heavy Industries
DESIGNATION: S-2 Traxus Cargo Transporter
CREW: 1 driver
LENGTH: 19.8ft (6.1m)
WIDTH: 7ft (2.1m)

Operator seat

Five-ton capacity

Hydraulic lift system

RELIABLE MACHINERY

The S-2 forklift was designed by Traxus Heavy Industries in 2538 to replace the S-1 models which had been the subject of personal injury lawsuits filed on Earth, Tribute, and Skopje. As a consequence of the suits, the newest model included both a kill switch and safety sensor, among a handful of other alterations. The forklift's mechanism and function has changed little over the five hundred years they have been around: They remain slow, sturdy, and effective at their incredibly simple task.

FORWARD UNTO DAWN
UNSC FORWARD UNTO DAWN FFG-201

The UNSC *Forward Unto Dawn*, commanded by Miranda Keyes, is part of the Seventh Fleet, a collection of ships brought back from the frontlines of the Covenant War to defend planet Earth.

STATISTICS

HALO 3 • HALO 3: ODST

Forward Unto Dawn can be seen throughout Halo 3's campaign, providing the Master Chief with weapons, equipment and transportation as he brought the war against the Covenant to an end.

REGISTRY: FFG-201
CLASS: *Charon*-class Light Frigate
FLEET: Seventh Fleet
COMMANDING OFFICER: Miranda Keyes
LENGTH: 1,607ft (490m)
BEAM: 510ft (156m)
PRIMARY ARMAMENT:
Magnetic Accelerator Cannon
SECONDARY ARMAMENT:
    Missile Delivery System
    TERTIARY ARMAMENT:
        Point Defense System

HEAVY CARGO

Charon-class frigates like the *Dawn* have larger hangar bays than *Stalwart*-class frigates for ferrying sizeable matériel during ground engagements.

MAC

Primary bay

Point Defense System

ASSAULT ON THE ARK

On November 17, 2552, the *Forward Unto Dawn* participated in the assault against the Prophet of Truth's dreadnought as it attempted to activate an ancient Forerunner Portal. When this attack proved unsuccessful, Miranda Keyes ordered the *Dawn* to follow the Covenant to the Ark, leading the fight against their enemy one last time. After achieving victory, the frigate attempted to return home safely only to be shorn apart by the closing slipspace Portal, leaving the fate of the Master Chief unknown.

Commander Miranda Keyes helmed two vessels at the end of the Covenant War: *In Amber Clad* and *Forward Unto Dawn*.

FRAG GRENADE

M9 HIGH EXPLOSIVE-DUAL PURPOSE ANTIPERSONNEL GRENADE

The M9 is composed of approximately six ounces of ComL, a chemical compound triggered by a digital timer fuse when activated.

The M9 HE-DP is the primary grenade solution for all branches of the UNSC. It provides a quick, simple, and most effective option for clearing infantry, drawing out dug-in enemies, or dropping the shielding of an Elite.

TRADITIONAL EXPLOSIVES

Not revolutionary in the least, the M9 HE-DP is yet another example of military technology standing the test of time and the strain of battle. The UNSC holds an array of M9 antipersonnel fragmentation options, but most perform with similar efficacy. Unlike the Covenant's primary T-1 APG, the frag grenade can be used to ricochet off hard objects and work around fortified structures, which has made it particularly valuable over the course of the Covenant War.

STATISTICS

HALO: COMBAT EVOLVED
HALO 2 • HALO 3 • HALO WARS
HALO 3: ODST • HALO: REACH

The frag grenade's hard shell allows skilled players to ricochet it off walls and floors, sending deadly explosive into areas other grenades cannot reach.

MANUFACTURER: Misriah Armory
DESIGNATION: M9 High Explosive-Dual Purpose Antipersonnel Grenade
FILLER: ComL
FILLER AMOUNT: 6.7oz (190g)
DIAMETER: 3.7in (9.4cm)
KILLING RADIUS: 16ft (5m)
CASUALTY RADIUS: 49.2ft (15m)

Digital timer fuse

Up-sized configuration

UP-SIZED FOR SPARTANS

As with other matériel employed by the UNSC, some frag variants have been significantly "up-sized" for use by Spartans.

75

UNSC

FRIGATE
UNSC SHIP CLASSIFICATION

The frigate is one of the lighter ship groups employed by the UNSC. Primarily used for fast attack and escort operations, it is the most common vessel used in the war against the Covenant.

Bridge

Point Defense System

MAC

STATISTICS

HALO 2 • HALO 3 • HALO 3: ODST HALO: REACH

In Halo 3's Campaign mission "The Ark," players witness the rapid and impressive descent of the *Forward Unto Dawn* to the Ark's surface.

CLASS: *Stalwart* (Light Frigate)
  LENGTH: 1,568ft (478m)
   BEAM: 498ft (152m)
    ROLE: Defense, escort

  CLASS: *Charon* (Light Frigate)
  LENGTH: 1,607ft (490m)
   BEAM: 510ft (156m)
ROLE: Defense, escort

CLASS: *Paris* (Heavy Frigate)
LENGTH: 1,755ft (535m)
BEAM: 652ft (199m)
ROLE: Escort, attack

PRIMARY ARMAMENT:
Magnetic Accelerator Cannon
SECONDARY ARMAMENT:
Missile Delivery System
TERTIARY ARMAMENT:
Point Defense System

The UNSC *In Amber Clad* and the UNSC *Forward Unto Dawn* frigates had critical roles in the final battles of the Covenant War.

FRIGATE CLASSES

The UNSC frigate group includes an extensive selection of ships within multiple classes, the three most prominent being *Stalwart*, *Charon*, and *Paris*. Particularly common, especially within the context of planetary defense, are the *Stalwart* and *Charon* classes, as both are well-armed and extremely mobile. The heaviest frigates are those in the *Paris*-class, which are typically used as fleet escort but are also capable of directly engaging enemies whenever needed. Over the course of the war, frigates have played a major role in humanity's fight against the Covenant. They were present at the battle on Reach and they led the strike against the High Prophet of Truth's efforts to activate the Forerunner portal on Earth. Furthermore, it was the UNSC frigate *Forward Unto Dawn*, fighting alongside the Elites' *Fleet of Retribution* high above the surface of the Ark, which finally brought an end to the war.

FUEL ROD GUN
TYPE-33 LIGHT ANTI-ARMOR WEAPON

Capable of firing an explosive ballistic projectile, the shoulder-mounted Fuel Rod Gun is a Covenant weapon that has seen its fair share of design modifications, but its performance has remained spectacular.

38mm Fuel Rods

Range Dial

Cowling

The Fuel Rod Gun was first used against humans in 2531, six years after first contact with the Covenant.

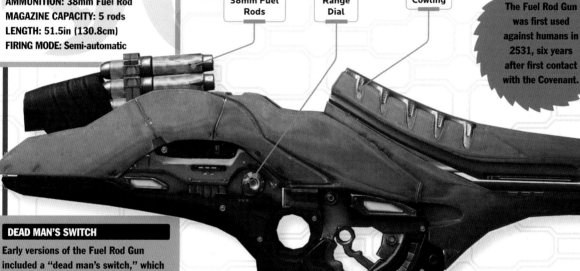

DEAD MAN'S SWITCH

Early versions of the Fuel Rod Gun included a "dead man's switch," which triggered a systemic, cascading mechanical failure upon the death of the user, suddenly detonating any remaining ammunition within the chamber.

Grip

ANTI-ARMOR EFFECTIVENESS

The recoil-operated, shoulder-mounted Type-33 Light Anti-Armor Weapon belongs to the same technology platform as other Covenant weapons using green, caseless explosive projectiles, which are often referred to as "fuel rods." It fires Class-2 38mm rods and is capable of launching them accurately up to 541ft (165m). The Fuel Rod Gun was designed for anti-armor purposes, though its overwhelming effectiveness against infantry (especially in groups) is unmatched compared to other anti-personnel weapons.

GAUSS WARTHOG

M12 LIGHT ANTI-ARMOR VEHICLE—GAUSS

The Gauss Warthog is a heavier variant of the standard M12 Warthog FAV, instead incorporating the M68 ALIM Gauss Cannon, which can fire 25 x 130mm rounds at hypersonic speeds.

STATISTICS

HALO 2 • HALO 3 • HALO WARS
HALO 3: ODST • HALO: REACH

The Gauss Hog first appeared in Halo 2 in 2004, and has appeared in every Halo game since.

MANUFACTURER: AMG Transport Dynamics
DESIGNATION: M12 Light Anti-Armor Vehicle—Gauss
CREW: 1 driver + 1 gunner + 1 passenger
LENGTH: 19.7ft (6m)
WIDTH: 9.9ft (3m)
PRIMARY ARMAMENT:
  M68 ALIM Gauss Cannon

Iterations of the Gauss Cannon have tried to balance mobility, visibility, and overall combat effectiveness.

M68 ALIM Gauss Cannon

360-degree swivel mount

All-terrain wheels

DEVELOPMENT HISTORY

The name "Gauss" originates from Carl Friedrich Gauss, a 19th century mathematician and physicist, whose work eventually led to the development of asynchronous linear-induction technology.

DEVASTATING FIREPOWER

The M12 Gauss Warthog performs the functionality offered by the M12 FAV base model, only with a much more powerful armament. Using an asynchronous linear-induction motor, the Gauss Hog can fire a high-density slug at heavy armor with hypersonic speeds approaching Mach 40. Such a vicious arsenal mounted onto such a versatile and mobile vehicle is nothing short of amazing.

UNSC

GHOST

TYPE-32 RAPID ATTACK VEHICLE

The Ghost is a remarkably versatile single-operator craft with an armament used for swift assaults on enemy fortifications and the capacity to perform scouting maneuvers with incredible efficiency.

SCOUTING TRADEOFF

The Ghost is one of the most common vehicles in the Covenant armament, despite its major flaw: the operator's exposure to enemy fire.

FIELDED BY SCOUTS

The Ghost marries incredible speed and mobility with a pair of plasma cannons, creating a threat to both enemy infantry and light vehicles. While the Ghost's armament favors rapid strikes and infantry support, the vehicle also performs admirably in a scouting role. Thanks to its relatively quiet operation and sleek, adaptable performance, it is used for reconnaissance, sent in advance of the Covenant's lines for scouting and intel gathering. Since the Ghost can reach relatively high speeds out in the open, it can be particularly devastating to high concentrations of enemy infantry.

Early versions of the Ghost were developed by the Elites pre- Covenant. It is now manufactured by the Iruiru Armory on Sanghelios.

Anti-gravity system

STATISTICS

HALO: COMBAT EVOLVED
HALO 2 • HALO 3 • HALO WARS
HALO 3: ODST • HALO: REACH

Targeting a Ghost's exposed fuel cell results in the destruction of the vehicle.

MANUFACTURER: Iruiru Armory
DESIGNATION: Type-32 Rapid Attack Vehicle
CREW: 1 operator
LENGTH: 13.8ft (4.2m)
WIDTH: 12.6ft (3.9m)
PRIMARY ARMAMENT:
Medium Plasma Cannon (2)

Plasma cannons

GRAFTON
UNSC GRAFTON FFG-318

The UNSC *Grafton* was one of a number of frigates present during the first stages of the Covenant's invasion of Reach. It became the first casualty of the ominous Covenant supercarrier, the *Long Night of Solace*.

STATISTICS

HALO: REACH

The UNSC *Grafton* can be seen throughout Halo: Reach's campaign mission "Tip of the Spear," where Noble Six is tasked with the elimination of several anti-air batteries throughout Szurdok Ridge.

REGISTRY: FFG-318
CLASS: *Paris*-class Heavy Frigate
FLEET: Epsilon Eridani Fleet
COMMANDING OFFICER:
Francis Mallarde
LENGTH: 1,755ft (535m)
BEAM: 652ft (199m)
PRIMARY ARMAMENT:
Magnetic Accelerator Cannon
SECONDARY ARMAMENT:
Missile Delivery System
TERTIARY ARMAMENT:
Point Defense System

ESCAPING DESTRUCTION

The *Grafton* was accompanied by a second frigate, *Saratoga*, which assisted in clearing out the local Covenant resistance. It narrowly escaped the *Long Night of Solace* when the *Grafton* was taken out.

MAC

Primary bay

Point Defense System

BATTLE AT SZURDOK

One of the *Paris*-class frigates within Epsilon Eridani's local fleet, the UNSC *Grafton* FFG-318 was one of only a few vessels available to confront the Covenant forces on Szurdok Ridge. After the UNSC Army eliminated much of the Covenant's resistance, the *Grafton* was ordered to assault one of the teleportation spires that the aliens were using to ferry infantry to the surface. The *Grafton* fired a MAC round directly at the spire, and although this shot destroyed the spire's teleportation system, the UNSC's victory was short-lived. Soon after, the Covenant's supercarrier *Long Night of Solace* used its ventral cleansing beam to bring down the *Grafton*, grinding the UNSC's progress to a halt.

GRAVEMIND
LF.XX.3273, COMPOUND INTELLIGENCE

STATISTICS

HALO 2 • HALO 3 • HALO WARS

In Halo 2, players encounter a Gravemind firsthand with the Master Chief and the Arbiter when the compound intelligence reveals exactly why Halo is so dangerous.

SPECIES: LF.Xx.3273 [FSC], *Inferi sententia*
TYPES/FORMS:
Proto-Gravemind
Gravemind

A Gravemind is the sentient embodiment of all individual Flood forms, both local and remote. It is an entity (or class of entities) that evolves to become the coordinating agent of the parasite's movement.

Tentacle

ORIGIN OF A GRAVEMIND

A Gravemind begins with the coalescence of raw, organic material (predominantly that of a sentient creature) and the fusion of the FCS, resulting in what is known as a Proto-Gravemind, an early precursor to the Gravemind itself.

Fleshy membrane

Once the Coordinated Stage is reached, a Gravemind can generate "pure" Flood forms directly from its FSC mass, ending its need for hosts.

THE COMPOUND MIND

Once a Flood outbreak has reached a specific threshold, it begins to aggregate its organic matter in order to establish a viable Gravemind, eventually fusing its LF.Xx.3273 [FSC], the Flood Super Cell. This process transitions the Flood from the "Feral Stage" into the "Coordinated Stage," allowing the Gravemind to communicate and control all Flood forms within its extensive range. It is here that the Flood truly becomes dangerous, as its once disparate parts can now work together strategically to spread the parasite to other worlds. A Gravemind is easily the most dangerous aspect of the Flood.

GRAVITY HAMMER
TYPE-2 ENERGY WEAPON/HAMMER

At the heart of the Brutes' armament of vicious weaponry lies the Gravity Hammer. Built for close-range melee combat, this weapon also serves as a ceremonial vestige of clan leadership for their species.

Tungsten-alloy blade

Gravity-drive

One of the most notorious Gravity Hammers is the *Fist of Rukt*, the weapon used by the infamous chieftain, Tartarus.

STATISTICS

HALO 2 • HALO 3 • HALO WARS
HALO 3: ODST • HALO: REACH

The Gravity Hammer is a lethal weapon which is particularly useful in environments with narrow corridors and hallways.

MANUFACTURER: Sacred Promissory
DESIGNATION: Type-2 Energy Weapon/Hammer
ENERGY CAPACITY: 100 units
LENGTH: 80.2in (203.7cm)

Grip

WEAPON PRODUCTION

During the early years of the war, the Brutes fashioned many of their weapons and vehicles on their own. However, the Sacred Promissory began producing such weapons en masse only a few months before the Great Schism.

CEREMONIAL WEAPON

In spite of its ceremonial significance, the Type-2 Energy Weapon/Hammer, also known as the Gravity Hammer, is clearly a war hammer: Its head is composed of a heavy base on one end and a razor-sharp blade on the other. Inside the head lies another component: a short-range gravity drive which can effectively and briefly displace local gravity. But not all hammers have the same appearance or function. Since the weapon maintains totemistic, ceremonial significance, some hammers have been aesthetically and operationally tailored for the particular uses of specific clans, families, or packs.

STATISTICS

HALO: COMBAT EVOLVED
HALO 2 • HALO 3 • HALO WARS
HALO 3: ODST • HALO: REACH

Grunts are the least dangerous enemy to face in combat, save for those armed with Fuel Rod Guns.

SPECIES: Unggoy, *Monachus Frigus*
AVERAGE HEIGHT: 65.7in (167cm)
AVERAGE WEIGHT: 260.1lbs (118kg)
HOMEWORLD: Balaho
TYPES/FORMS: Minor, Major, Heavy, SpecOps, Ultra, Deacon

The arthropod Grunts reside at the bottom of the Covenant hierarchy. With a large population and diminutive size, they by and large serve as manual laborers and, most often, cannon fodder.

Methane backpack

Rough skin

Breathing mask

CANNON FODDER

The Grunts were introduced into the Covenant relatively late. Their frigid, methane-rich homeworld, Balaho, had experienced an environmental catastrophe due to overindustrialization. The deteriorated ecology made life on their planet extremely difficult and so most Grunts openly welcomed the Covenant and the seemingly providential safety the alliance offered. But when it was time for the Covenant to incorporate the Grunt species into their ranks, these diminutive creatures were placed at the lowest end of the pecking order and are deployed en masse to overwhelm enemies with their sheer numbers.

GRUNT REBELLION

In 2462, feuding between the Grunts and Jackals peaked, leading the Grunts to rebel against the Covenant. In response, the Elites ruthlessly glassed large portions of Balaho—which put an end to the Grunt rebellion.

GUILTY SPARK
MONITOR OF INSTALLATION 04

The ancient AI construct known as 343 Guilty Spark was the Monitor of Alpha Halo. He maintained Halo and protected it from the Flood at any cost, following his Forerunner mandate to the very end.

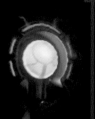

STATISTICS

HALO: COMBAT EVOLVED
HALO 2 • HALO 3

In Halo 3, Guilty Spark became the final enemy of the trilogy and players were tasked with his elimination, as well as the activation of Halo.

FULL NAME: 343 Guilty Spark (04-343)
ORIGIN: Forerunner
CLASS: Distributed Intelligence
ROLE: Monitor
AGE: 100,000 years (approx)
LOCATION: Installation 04 (Alpha Halo)
LENGTH: 22.9in (58.2cm)
WIDTH: 19.9in (50.6cm)

Lens

Anti-gravity mechanism

343 Guilty Spark is referred to by the Covenant as the "Oracle," an honorary name given to specific Forerunner AIs.

Directed energy conduit

SPARK AND HUMANITY

Guilty Spark's relationship with humanity has been odd and tenuous. He fought against them on the first Halo ring, but then joined their cause after the discovery of the second, only to betray them when they prepared to prematurely activate a third.

THE CARETAKER

After serving on Alpha Halo for over 100,000 years, the installation that was under 343 Guilty Spark's charge was destroyed by the Master Chief. Spark later joined humanity to prevent the firing of Delta Halo and led them to the Ark. There he discovered that the Ark was actually used by the Forerunners to build the original Halo rings. When a replacement of his original installation was once again being threatened by the humans, he betrayed them and was subsequently brought to an end by the Master Chief.

FORERUNNER

GUNGNIR ARMOR

MJOLNIR POWERED ASSAULT ARMOR/G—GUNGNIR

STATISTICS

HALO: REACH

Gungnir is available to players with the rank of Brigadier and for 250,000 credits in Halo: Reach's Armory.

SERIES: Mark V
MANUFACTURER: Misriah Armory
TESTING SITE: Rajtom Facility

A variant of MJOLNIR, Gungnir armor is designed to maximize target awareness and firing effectiveness when fielding the Spartan Laser. Its appearance on the battlefield is rare but always welcomed.

Blast visor

Wyrd III optimization

SPARTAN LASER

Gungnir utilizes Wyrd III synchronized optimization which seamlessly tethers the armor wearer to the Spartan Laser's full functionality.

Gungnir is one of only a few examples where MJOLNIR armor was modified to be paired with a specific weapon or vehicle.

Mk. V— undersuit mesh

TANDEM TECHNOLOGIES

GUNGNIR was one of several programs under the administration of Vice Admiral Hieronymus Michael Stanforth, and one that dovetailed heavily into both MJOLNIR and SPARTAN-II. While designing the M6 Grindell/Galilean Nonlinear Rifle, also commonly known as the Spartan Laser, a separate but parallel team worked on its integration with MJOLNIR. Gungnir is simply a modification of existing MJOLNIR sighting/ target-tracking technologies that gives a soldier the ability to fire the nonlinear rifle more effectively (particularly while in motion).

HALSEY
CATHERINE ELIZABETH HALSEY, M.D., PH.D.

Unparalleled in her many fields of expertise, Doctor Catherine Halsey believed that the only way to stop the ominous threat of colonial rebellion was to create a solution which was equally ominous.

A BRILLIANT MIND

To deal with the mounting civil war, Doctor Halsey initiated the SPARTAN-II and MJOLNIR projects. These aimed to engineer soldiers unmatched in speed, strength, and combat effectiveness. But before the finished product could be fielded against rebels, the Covenant struck mercilessly and Halsey's Spartans were forced to fight against them for three decades. Halsey's work also led her to discover the ancient Forerunner civilization, which eventually revealed the Forerunner legacy passed down to humanity.

Security badge

ONI parka

Although it is not widely known, Doctor Halsey's daughter is the young but formidable Commander Miranda Keyes.

STATISTICS

HALO: REACH

Halsey plays an integral role in Halo's backstory and appears in Halo: Reach's "ONI: Sword Base" and "The Package."

FULL NAME: Catherine Elizabeth Halsey
SERVICE NUMBER: CC-409871
BRANCH: UNSC Navy
GROUP: Office of Naval Intelligence, Section Three
HEIGHT: 5ft 7in (170.2cm)
WEIGHT: 125lbs (56.7kg)
HOMEWORLD: Reach
DATE OF BIRTH: March 19, 2492
DATE OF DEATH: [CLASSIFIED]

BIRTH OF CORTANA

Dr. Halsey cloned herself in order to create the smart AI construct known as Cortana.

SUPERCONTINENT

Harvest's primary landmass is the enormous and fertile supercontinent of Edda.

For almost a century, Harvest was a major exporter of agricultural goods throughout all human-controlled space—until it became the first of many colonies to be destroyed by the Covenant in 2525.

THE FIRST TO FALL

In 2525, the agrarian colony of Harvest was suddenly assaulted by the Covenant. For several months, the fate of the colony remained a mystery, but in 2526, Vice Admiral Preston Cole arrived with one of the largest fleets ever assembled. Despite incredible losses, he reclaimed the planet, but his fleet became entrenched in a vicious battle that lasted over five years. In 2531, an ancient artifact buried below the planet's surface finally ended the Covenant's occupation of Harvest and began to open humanity's eyes to the secrets of the Forerunners.

Diameter:
2,493 miles
(4,012km)

STATISTICS

HALO WARS

The first three missions of Halo Wars take place entirely on Harvest.

STAR, POSITION: Epsilon Indi, IV
SATELLITE(S): None
GRAVITY: 0.998 G (approx)
ATMOSPHERE: 1.02 (N_2, O_2)
SURFACE TEMPERATURE: −2°F to 108°F (−19°C to 42°C)
DATE FOUNDED: 2468
MAJOR CITIES: Gladsheim, Tigard, Utgard
POPULATION: 3,000,000 (pre-war)
SPACE TETHERS: 7

Prior to its fall, Harvest's seven tethers were connected to the orbital space station Tiara and managed by the AI construct Sif.

HAZOP ARMOR

MJOLNIR POWERED ASSAULT ARMOR—HAZARD OPERABILITY (HAZOP)

Alongside the abundant variants of Mark V armor being developed by the Materials Group came HAZOP, an armor specifically crafted to endure extremely volatile environmental conditions.

While all MJOLNIR armor has radiation shielding, HAZOP utilizes a specialized material to protect from heightened exposure.

IMPROVED PROTECTION

Hazard Operability (HAZOP) armor was deployed alongside a slew of MJOLNIR Mark V variants, but its history extends much further back in the Covenant War. Prototypes of the suit were fielded in the years prior to its launch, as the UNSC met the Covenant head-on in environments that were chemically volatile or were otherwise inhospitable. When "traditional" MJOLNIR armor failed to meet the requirements in these extreme conditions, HAZOP quickly proved to be the best solution, and one which remained effective until the end of the Covenant War.

UA/bracer

HAZOP pauldron

STATISTICS

HALO: REACH

HAZOP is one of the first variants available in Halo: Reach's Armory. It costs 7,000 credits and requires the rank of Recruit.

SERIES: Mark V
MANUFACTURER: Materials Group
TESTING SITE: Damascus Materials Testing Facility

EXTREME CONDITIONS

HAZOP employs a unique technology to process and manufacture oxygen in highly toxic conditions, allowing significantly longer deployments in otherwise deadly environments.

UA/Chobham

HIGH CHARITY
THE COVENANT HOLY CITY

For the Prophets, High Charity replaced their homeworld, which had been the victim of a stellar collapse in 648 BCE.

Built around the Forerunner Dreadnought, the enormous space station known as High Charity was the Covenant homeworld that once carried millions of its diverse inhabitants across the galaxy.

CHARITY'S END

When the High Prophet of Truth brought High Charity to Delta Halo, the Flood found its way onboard and rapidly infected the city's population. Amid this chaos, Truth escaped with the Forerunner Dreadnought, leaving the High Charity's citizens to fend for themselves. Eventually, High Charity met its end when the Gravemind crashed it into the Ark in an attempt to prevent the firing of the Halo Array.

Diameter: 216 miles (348km)

STATISTICS

HALO 2 • HALO 3

In Halo 3's mission "Cortana," players must infiltrate the Flood-infested High Charity and destroy it by overloading the city's last active reactor core.

GRAVITY: 0.95 G (approx)
ATMOSPHERE: 1.03 (N_2, O_2, Ar)
SURFACE TEMPERATURE: 50°F to 75°F (10°C to 24°C)
DATE FOUNDED: 648 BCE
MAJOR SITES: High Council Chamber, Sanctum of the Hierarchs, Tower Districts, Lower Districts
POPULATION: 23,831,346 (pre-war)
UMBILICAL TETHERS: 8,930

HIDDEN WITHIN

High Charity's vast umbilical docking system and reinforced structural composition hide an immense interior filled with atmosphere, light, and life.

Umbilical docking system

While the Covenant are led by the High Prophet triumvirate, the High Council is a larger ruling body of both Prophets and Elites that determines legislation and executes all the affairs of the government.

STATISTICS

HALO 2

The High Councilors are first seen in the opening act of Halo 2 when the commander Thel 'Vadamee is placed on trial for the destruction of Halo.

SPECIES: San'Shyuum and Sangheili
LOCATION: High Council Chamber, High Charity
FUNCTION: Political affairs, governance, administrative consultation

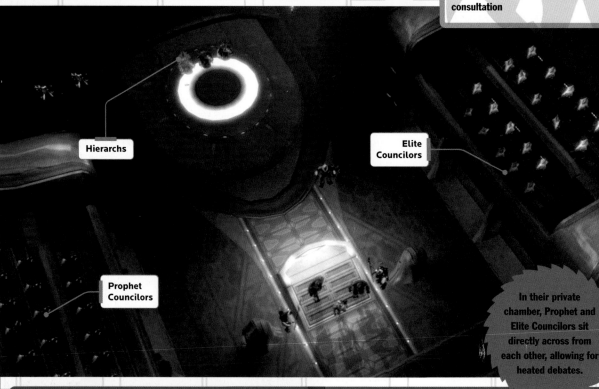

Hierarchs

Elite Councilors

Prophet Councilors

In their private chamber, Prophet and Elite Councilors sit directly across from each other, allowing for heated debates.

THE RULING BODY

Although the Covenant maintain an imperial theocracy with the Hierarch triumvirate at its zenith, the High Council is the leading governing body and the primary source of all decision-making. This group of over 200 Prophets and Elites not only manages the governance of the Covenant, but it is also responsible for selecting the replacements of any Hierarch if deemed necessary. For this reason, when the High Prophet of Truth replaced the Honor Guard with Brutes, he moved quickly, ordering the execution of all the Elites on the High Council. This initiated the Great Schism, a civil war which eventually saw the end not only of the High Council but of the Covenant itself.

HONOR GUARD
SANCTUM OF THE HIERARCHS, HIGH CHARITY

Honor Guards do not always wear elaborate armor. They may eschew the heavy, cumbersome array for something more functional.

The three Prophet Hierarchs select the most esteemed Elite warriors to serve in their Honor Guard. These handpicked few swear loyalty only to the High Prophets and protect them, even unto death.

Ornate helmet

High Council Chamber

STATISTICS

HALO 2 • HALO WARS

The "Changing of the Guard" is a pivotal moment in Halo 2. This occurs right before the player, as the Arbiter, is sent on a mission to procure the Sacred Icon.

SPECIES: Sangheili and Jiralhanae
LOCATION: Sanctum of the Hierarchs, High Charity
FUNCTION: Escort and protection of the Hierarchs
ARMAMENT: Energy Stave

Elaborate ceremonial armor

REPLACED BY BRUTES

When the Honor Guards were formed to protect the Hierarch triumvirate, the select few could only be the most skilled and experienced Elites. Toward the end of the Covenant War, however, the Prophet of Truth controversially altered that. Believing the Elites to be a threat, and having already forged a secret alliance with the Brutes, Truth changed the Honor Guard to the more savage, albeit loyal, Jiralhanae. This act turned the Elites against the Covenant and they, alongside humanity, brought an end to Truth and the last vestige of the Brute Honor Guard.

CEREMONIAL ROLE

While it is a great privilege to serve on the Honor Guard, it is a largely ceremonial unit which sees relatively little combat, if any at all. A few Elites have declined this promotion.

COVENANT

HORNET
AV-14 HORNET

There are few more efficient rapid assault and reconnaissance vehicles than the Hornet. In a wide-ranging fleet of VTOL crafts, it holds its own in everything from close air support and escort to covert infantry deployment.

The Hornet has been in use for years, playing roles in military campaigns as far back as TREBUCHET.

GUA-23/A Heavy Autocannons

Class-2 GMLS

Skids

STATISTICS

HALO 3 • HALO WARS

The Hornet's most effective armament is the guided munition system, where the operator must lock onto a target.

MANUFACTURER: Misriah Armory
DESIGNATION: AV-14 Hornet
CREW: 1 pilot + 4 passengers
LENGTH: 31.4ft (9.6m)
WIDTH: 28.5ft (8.7m)
PRIMARY ARMAMENT:
GUA-23/A Heavy Autocannon (2)
SECONDARY ARMAMENT: Class-2
Guided Munition Launch System

FAST ATTACK VTOL

Some UNSC flying vehicles are designed to exclusively engage airborne enemies and others only deploy infantry units, but the Hornet deftly juggles both roles. While it is capable at providing air combat support and escorting high-value assets, its dual skids provide hard points for up to four passengers at a time. The Hornet's main arsenal is based on Class-2 GMLS technology: Twin missile launchers fire homing ordnance, supported by a pair of high-mounted GUA-23/A Heavy Autocannons.

HUNTERS
MGALEKGOLO

STATISTICS

HALO: COMBAT EVOLVED • HALO 2
HALO 3 • HALO WARS
HALO 3: ODST • HALO: REACH

In Halo: Combat Evolved, the Hunter only requires one carefully placed shot in order to fall.

SPECIES: Mgalekgolo, *Ophis congregatio*
AVERAGE HEIGHT: 12ft 1in (368.7cm) (varies by individual)
AVERAGE WEIGHT: 10,500lbs (4,800kg) (varies by individual)
HOMEWORLD: Te

A Hunter is not a single organism, but rather a cohesive colony of eel-like creatures known as Lekgolo, all encased in a metal suit. They form the largest known infantry unit within the Covenant military.

Mgalekgolo colony

Individual Lekgolo were used to probe and explore the Forerunner Dreadnought's vast information pathways.

TAMING OF THE HUNTERS

Hunters in their current form were created by the Covenant. When the alliance arrived on the planet Te, they encountered the Lekgolo, an intelligent eel-like creature which devoured Forerunner artifacts. The Covenant failed to annihilate the Lekgolo, so the Elites decided to tame them instead. Fusing heavy armor and weapons onto the creatures when their colonies were tightly formed (a state known as "Mgalekgolo"), these beasts became Hunters, enormous, hulking units with incredible strength and resilience.

Armored shell

Heavy shield

FORM MEETS FUNCTION
Mgalekgolo have no standard size; their armor guides the formation and contours of their colonies.

97

IN AMBER CLAD
UNSC IN AMBER CLAD FFG-142

Helmed by Commander Miranda Keyes, the UNSC frigate *In Amber Clad* followed the Covenant's *Solemn Penance* into slipspace and arrived at Delta Halo; the site of a pivotal battle toward the end of the Covenant War.

Bridge

Propulsion system

Miranda Keyes became the commanding officer of *In Amber Clad* in April 2550.

New Mombasa

REMAINING BEHIND

Cortana was prepared to detonate the *Clad*'s fusion reactors, to prevent the Covenant from activating Delta Halo.

FEARLESS PURSUIT

Docked at Cairo Station when the Covenant first arrived at Earth on October 20, 2552, *In Amber Clad* played an instrumental part in the final weeks of the war. The frigate followed the Covenant's *Solemn Penance* to Delta Halo, hunting down the Prophet of Regret and engaging the local Covenant forces. During the course of this battle, *In Amber Clad* fell prey to a Flood outbreak on the ring's surface, finally impaling itself into the interior wall of High Charity, where it was eventually destroyed.

STATISTICS

HALO 2 • HALO: REACH

Despite Ivory Tower's versatility with all gametypes, Slayer dominated this elegant environment in both Team and Free-For-All modes.

ENVIRONMENT: Skyscraper Interior
RELEVANCE: New Mombasa Public Park, SinoViet Penthouse
LAYOUT: Multi-tiered room, ramps, corridors
PLAYER COUNT: 2 to 8
KEY WEAPONS: Sniper Rifle, Rocket Launcher, Energy Sword

First appearing in Halo 2, Ivory Tower is a tranquil indoor public park at the apex of one of New Mombasa's skyscrapers. Despite its serene aesthetic, its success lies in frenetic multiplayer violence.

REFLECTION

Given that Halo 2's Ivory Tower was a public park for the upper echelon of New Mombasa society, it was logical that Reflection was a penthouse in Reach's opulent New Alexandria.

ELEGANT ARENA

With wood flooring spanning a sun-dappled, flora-laden sanctuary, Halo 2's Ivory Tower and its Halo: Reach remake, Reflection, showcase some of the greatest multiplayer experiences Halo has offered. The map is girded by walkways, ramps, and lifts, and is overlooked by a large balcony at its far end. On the main floor players can find the Rocket Launcher, on the balcony the Sniper, and in the lower levels of the map, they can seize the Energy Sword. Ivory Tower's open yet protected spaces and its long lines of sight have made this a treat for Halo fans for years.

JACKALS
KIG-YAR

Mercenaries and pirates by nature, Jackals are more interested in the real world profitability of an endeavor rather than the spiritual ramifications of it. This approach informs their pragmatic view of their role within the Covenant.

STATISTICS

HALO: COMBAT EVOLVED
HALO 2 • HALO 3 • HALO WARS
HALO 3: ODST • HALO: REACH

Jackals typically fight from the protection of their point defense gauntlet. Firing at the Jackal's free hand can cause them to recoil, exposing their heads for an easy kill.

SPECIES: Kig-Yar, *Perosus latrunculus*
HEIGHT: 6ft 2in to 6ft 8in
(190cm to 203cm)
WEIGHT: 195lbs to 206lbs
(88kg to 93kg)
HOMEWORLD: Eayn
TYPES/FORMS: Minor, Major, Sniper, Ranger, Zealot, Shipmaster, Shipmistress

Tactical display

Sniper helmet

PIRATES AND MERCENARIES

The early history of the Jackal species was plagued with feuding and raids, which were only mitigated when clans began to intermingle. Likely due to their innate pragmatism, individual cultures merged and their technological prowess increased exponentially, which led the Jackals to intersystem colonization. It was then that they reverted to the looting and pillaging behavior of their ancestors. When the Covenant arrived, fleets belonging to the Jackal pirates were their only defense against this newfound enemy, but even those ruthless fleets paled against their aggressor's overwhelming force. The Jackals accepted roles within the Covenant and have been rewarded exceptionally well, despite their lack of zeal and fervency of faith.

T-31 Rifle

Eayn, the Jackals' homeworld, is the primary moon of Chu'ot, the third planet in the Y'Deio system.

Avian posture

STATISTICS

HALO: REACH

In Halo: Reach's Armory, the JFO armor is available with the rank of Lieutenant Colonel and for the cost of 60,000 credits.

SERIES: Mark V
MANUFACTURER: Beweglichrüstungsysteme
TESTING SITE: SWC Essen

Joint Fires Observer (JFO) is a MJOLNIR armor variant that improves artillery request communication/coordination by Spartans across the Army, Navy, and Marine Corps.

H-165 FOM

FORWARD OBSERVER MODULE

In addition to the standard arsenal for their specific branch, JFO Spartans also carry an H-165 Forward Observer Module, which is smart-linked to their MJOLNIR armor for target acquisition.

JFO-armored Spartans' central function is to direct artillery fire, which can take them into hostile territory.

Tactical/ Hard case

Tactical/ Recon kits

BEHIND ENEMY LINES

Despite the fact that most Spartan units are close-knit detachments of three to six soldiers, it is not uncommon to find single Spartans fielded in roles which involve reconnaissance, infiltration, and artillery targeting. JFO is one of these instances, and Spartans who don this armor are usually involved in combat scenarios that demand their presence well within heavily occupied territory. Spartans using JFO armor are equipped with a variety of systems and programs that not only conceal and protect them, but increase access and visibility to close air, orbital, and planetside artillery support.

JOHNSON
SERGEANT MAJOR AVERY JOHNSON

With decades of exemplary service in the UNSC, Sergeant Major Avery Johnson was ready to play a critical role in the fall of 2552, where he fought alongside the Master Chief until the Covenant's empire crumbled.

Johnson's Career Service Vitae (CSV) holds a litany of top-secret, highly classified military operations.

Sweet William cigar

GRIZZLED VETERAN

Johnson's lifelong service in the marines was almost unparalleled. He served in the highly classified ORION project, the rebellion-battering TREBUCHET campaign and was involved in the first contact with the Covenant near Harvest. After 27 years of fighting the alien alliance, Johnson fought across two Halo installations and the Ark, finally sacrificing his own life in a battle against the rampant Forerunner AI Guilty Spark, helping to protect humanity from the threat of the Flood and the Halo Array.

Protective collar

MA5C Assault Rifle

Marine BDU

STATISTICS

HALO: COMBAT EVOLVED • HALO 2 HALO 3 • HALO 3: ODST

Players could play as Sergeant Johnson for the first time in Halo 3: ODST's Firefight mode.

FULL NAME: Avery Junior Johnson
SERVICE NUMBER: 48789-20114-AJ
BRANCH: UNSC Marine Corps
GROUP: [CLASSIFIED]
RANK: Sergeant Major
HEIGHT: 6ft 2in (187.2cm)
WEIGHT: 210lbs (95.5kg)
HOMEWORLD: Earth
DATE OF BIRTH: [CLASSIFIED]
DATE OF DEATH: December 11, 2552

SKILLED SNIPER

Sergeant Johnson was a man of many talents within the Marine Corps, his most well-known skill was as an experienced sniper.

STATISTICS

HALO: REACH

In Halo: Reach's mission "Long Night of Solace," players accompany Jorge on a mission to take out the supercarrier.

FULL NAME: Jorge-052
SERVICE NUMBER: S-052
BRANCH: UNSC Army
GROUP: Special Warfare, Group Three
RANK: Chief Warrant Officer
HEIGHT: 7ft 4in (223.5cm)
WEIGHT: 320lbs (145.2kg)
HOMEWORLD: Reach
DATE OF BIRTH: March 5, 2511
DATE OF DEATH:
August 14, 2552

At a young age, Jorge was abducted by the Office of Naval Intelligence and crafted into an elite super-soldier within the SPARTAN-II program. He eventually came to serve as a member of Noble Team.

CUSTOMIZED ARMOR

Jorge made heavy modifications to his MJOLNIR Mark IV armor to suit his overall combat style and improve effectiveness.

Native to the planet Reach, Jorge is fluent in the local language and can effectively communicate with its civilians.

Mk. IV/
LBE–AA
Field Case

Mk. IV—UA/
Grenadier

UA Collar/
Pauldron

M247H
Heavy
Machine
Gun

Boot
guard

IN DEFENSE OF REACH

Like others in the SPARTAN-II program, Jorge was trained from childhood to be an augmented soldier of unequalled value. He fought against the Covenant and the insurrectionists for decades, later finding placement on the Special Warfare group codenamed "Noble." As Noble Five, this career soldier served in many military campaigns, culminating in a return to his home planet of Reach. On August 14, 2552, Jorge died in defense of this planet, manually triggering a slipspace event near the Covenant supercarrier *Long Night of Solace*.

JUN
WARRANT OFFICER JUN-A266, SPARTAN-III

An expert marksman and seasoned warrior, Jun-A266 is one of SPARTAN-III Alpha Company's best assets. Handpicked to serve on Noble Team, he fought the Covenant on the planet Reach.

SRS99 AM

STATISTICS

HALO: REACH

In the Halo: Reach mission "Nightfall," the player accompanies Jun on a scouting mission along Szurdok Ridge.

FULL NAME: Jun-A266
SERVICE NUMBER: S-A266
BRANCH: UNSC Army
GROUP: Special Warfare, Group Three
RANK: Warrant Officer
HEIGHT: 6ft 11in (210.5cm)
WEIGHT: 244.9lbs (111.1kg)
HOMEWORLD: New Harmony
DATE OF BIRTH: February 28, 2524

Jun-A266 was born in the city of Tyumen on New Harmony, which is also home to his teammate Kat-B320.

Combat knife

WEAPONRY

Jun's weapon of choice, as a scout and marksman, is the SRS99AM Sniper Rifle.

SEASONED SCOUT

Confident and skilled, Spartan Jun-A266 served on the Special Warfare group's elite Noble Team. In July 2552, Noble was called back to Reach, where it discovered a Covenant invasion force. As Noble Three, Jun-A266 bravely defended the planet until he and what was left of his team were ordered to Sword Base. It was there, deep below the ONI facility, that he learned of Dr. Halsey's Forerunner research. He was then ordered to split off from Noble team and escort Halsey to the relative safety of Castle Base. Though he was successful in his mission, Jun's ultimate fate remains a mystery.

KAT

STATISTICS

HALO: REACH

As Noble Six, players fight alongside Kat-B320 in the Halo: Reach missions "ONI: Sword Base" and "Tip of the Spear."

FULL NAME: Catherine-B320
SERVICE NUMBER: S-B320
BRANCH: UNSC Army
GROUP: Special Warfare, Group Three
RANK: Lieutenant Commander
HEIGHT: 6ft 9in (205.7cm)
WEIGHT: 215lbs (97.5kg)
HOMEWORLD: New Harmony
DATE OF BIRTH: January 30, 2530
DATE OF DEATH: August 23, 2552

Kat-B320, like other Spartans, was no stranger to the frontlines of the Covenant War. An expert cryptanalyst and brilliant tactician, Kat's skills were a critical component of Noble Team's effectiveness.

Mk.V—AA/FC-1

Cybernetic prosthesis

THE SACRIFICE

Born on New Harmony, Kat was kidnapped as a child and conscripted into the SPARTAN-III program. During the training process she was earmarked by Lieutenant Commander Kurt Ambrose due to her skill and was withdrawn from combat shortly before Operation: TORPEDO, which resulted in the deaths of nearly all of Beta Company. Kat was placed on Noble Team, under the leadership of Commander Carter-A259, and there she excelled in tactical intelligence and data retrieval. When the Covenant assaulted Reach, Kat lost her life while defending the devastated city of New Alexandria.

BATTLE OF FUMIROLE

Kat received her prosthetic arm after the battle for the colony of Fumirole, in which she attempted to plant a bomb on a Covenant cruiser.

KEYES, JACOB
CAPTAIN JACOB KEYES

There are few men or women within the UNSC Navy who have shown the level of fortitude, valor, and courage that Captain Jacob Keyes has displayed over the last three decades of his military service.

Keyes commanded a number of UNSC ships during his career, including the *Midsummer Night*, the *Iroquois* and the *Pillar of Autumn*.

Captain rank

Cortana

UNWAVERING BRAVERY

After a brief and daring skirmish near Sigma Octanus IV, Jacob Keyes was awarded the rank of captain and the UNSC granted a rare victory in the war. Only weeks later, he was pitted against the Covenant above the planet Reach and then at Halo, where he ultimately found his end in the clutches of the Flood. Nevertheless, Keyes' actions repeatedly proved his loyalty not only to the UNSC, but to all of humanity.

FAMILY LEGACY

Despite his impressive military career, Keyes' best legacy is his daughter, Miranda Keyes, who played an integral role in the final few battles of the Covenant War.

UNSC

KEYES, MIRANDA
COMMANDER MIRANDA KEYES

STATISTICS

HALO 2 • HALO 3

Miranda Keyes' voice can be heard in the Pelican radio chatter of Halo 3's "The Ark."

FULL NAME: Miranda Keyes
SERVICE NUMBER: 15972-19891-MK
BRANCH: UNSC Navy
GROUP: Home Fleet, Medii Battle Group
RANK: Commander
HEIGHT: 5ft 10in (177.8cm)
WEIGHT: 151lbs (68.5kg)
HOMEWORLD: Luna
DATE OF BIRTH: February 28, 2525
DATE OF DEATH: December 11, 2552

Commander Miranda Keyes defied skeptics by refusing to live in the shadow of her father. She bravely fought the Covenant in numerous battles, ultimately dying a hero as the UNSC brought the war to a close.

IMPRESSIVE CAREER

Keyes served on a number of ships in the UNSC Navy, including the *Hilbert* and the *Forward Unto Dawn*.

Commander rank

HER FATHER'S DAUGHTER

Despite a close relationship with her father, the highly regarded Jacob Keyes, Commander Miranda Keyes' military career did not come easy, and she was constantly hounded by charges of nepotism. During the final battles of the Covenant War, Keyes challenged all criticism when she twice pursued Covenant forces into slipspace from Earth. Her bravery contributed to the UNSC's victory against the Covenant, yet she did not live to see it. Keyes was killed by the Prophet of Truth, sacrificing her life to save a fellow soldier.

Miranda's parents Jacob Keyes and Catherine Halsey met in 2517, while secretly evaluating candidates for the SPARTAN-II project.

Regulation uniform

UNSC

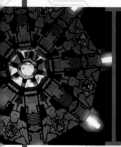

The Library is a structure on select Forerunner installations holding a vast database of information, but this is not its main function. At the heart of a Halo's Library site is the Activation Index—the key to firing the Array.

STATISTICS

HALO: COMBAT EVOLVED • HALO 2

In Halo 2's mission "Sacred Icon," the Library is the site where the Arbiter is betrayed by Tartarus and the High Prophets.

DESIGNATION: Archive Complex and Research Facility
SITES: Forerunner installations
FUNCTION: Contains Forerunner records and the Activation Index
COMPOSITION: Enormous facility with a vast, multi-tiered interior network

Sentinel factory

Delta Halo's library

Library sites are not exclusive to Halo installations, though their purpose and function on other constructs may differ.

Ground entrance

FLOOD PROTECTION

To prevent entry by the Flood, most Library sites are extravagantly sectioned off from the remainder of the installation by way of a moat, chasm, or in some cases, an enormous wall.

ACTIVATION INDEX

Deep within this vast research facility and archive complex is the Activation Index. While the information within the Library is something of a mystery, the Index's purpose is not. It is the mechanism by which a Halo ring is activated, making it the most significant threat to the Flood. And, unsurprisingly, the Library is the first place the parasite attempts to attack during the course of an outbreak. Activation of the Halo rings can only be initiated by a human, or "Reclaimer," inserting the Index into the activation console in the Control Room. Next to the Control Room, the Library is easily a Halo ring's most important site.

STATISTICS

HALO 2 • HALO 3

Despite its size and asymmetry, Lockout is one of the most popular Halo multiplayer maps for almost any gametype.

ENVIRONMENT: Highly lofted platform structure
RELEVANCE: Forerunner Research Site, Weather Station
LAYOUT: Asymmetrical platforms and rooms
PLAYER COUNT: 4 to 12
KEY WEAPONS: Shotgun, Energy Sword, Sniper Rifle

Incredibly simple in design and layout, Lockout was the most frequently played map in Halo 2. The environment proved that brilliantly crafted places sometimes come from the simplest spaces.

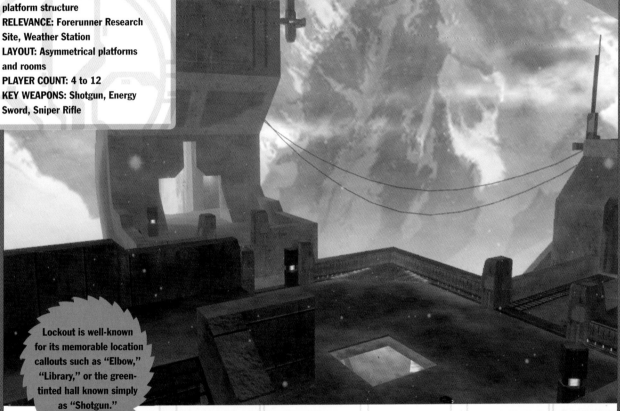

Lockout is well-known for its memorable location callouts such as "Elbow," "Library," or the green-tinted hall known simply as "Shotgun."

PERFECT PLATFORMS

At first glance, Lockout appears to be empty, simple, and somewhat bland. However, the central platform and the series of rooms, ramps, and lifts girding it have become the source of some of the most addictive multiplayer combat ever to grace Halo's history. Players cherished this map and memorized it to an insane level of detail, leveraging this knowledge within the game's rich physics and sandbox to create an experience that was not only infinitely replayable but also simply amazing. In Halo 3, this cherished map returned as Blackout.

LOCUST
TYPE-30 LIGHT EXCAVATION/ANTI-FORTIFICATION PLATFORM

Originally built for the Covenant's excavation needs on worlds where traditional mining methods were not successful, the Locust was later repurposed to serve as an anti-fortification vehicle against humanity.

Other than size and general design, the principle difference between the Locust and the Scarab is that the latter is formed of Lekgolo colonies.

WAR UPGRADE

During the war, the Locust was upgraded to incorporate some of the Covenant's preexisting shield technology, reinforcing its use as a combat vehicle.

Operator cabin

Heavy Plasma Cannon

Nimble legs

STATISTICS

HALO WARS

In Halo Wars, the Locust is an incredible asset against enemy bases, firing a constant and destructive beam of plasma.

MANUFACTURER: Assembly Forges
DESIGNATION: Type-30 Light Excavation/Anti-Fortification Platform
CREW: 1 operator
LENGTH: 19ft (5.8m)
WIDTH: 39.4ft (12m)
PRIMARY ARMAMENT:
Charged Plasma Cannon

VERSATILE EXCAVATOR

While the inner workings of the single-manned Locust differ dramatically from its older and larger brother, the Scarab, it too was originally designed to excavate Forerunner relics. The Locust can be deployed into difficult environments using its heavy plasma cannon to mine geological sites and unearth artifacts from even the most dug-in of reliquaries. During the Covenant War, the Locust was used as an ad hoc anti-fortification platform, capable of eliminating infantry and vehicles, and leveling entire UNSC bases.

STATISTICS

HALO: REACH

In Halo: Reach's "Long Night of Solace," the player climbs into the skies of Reach to assault this supercarrier, destroying it with a slipspace drive.

CLASS: CSO (Supercarrier)
FLEET: Fleet of Valiant Prudence
SHIPMASTER: Rho 'Barutamee
LENGTH: 95,014ft (28,960m)
BEAM: 37,566ft (11,447m)
PRIMARY ARMAMENT:
Ventral Cleansing Beam
SECONDARY ARMAMENT:
Anterior Plasma Cannons
TERTIARY ARMAMENT:
Point Laser Defense

Most of humanity was unaware of the Covenant's presence on Reach until August 30, 2552, but the *Long Night of Solace* had already been conducting a more discrete invasion in the empty canyons of Szurdok Ridge.

THE HIDDEN INVASION

Despite its enormous size, the *Solace* was quite capable of masking itself and all of Valiant Prudence's presence to the vast majority of Reach.

Propulsion system

Ventral Cleansing Beam

Gravity lift

POWERFUL SUPERCARRIER

Arriving at Reach shortly after the battle for Sigma Octanus IV, the *Long Night of Solace* secretly penetrated the planet's defenses, took out a major communications relay, and ferried large numbers of troops and equipment to the surface. It was discovered when the UNSC located teleportation/interference spires spread throughout Szurdok Ridge and attempted to take one out. Eventually, the *Solace* was destroyed during Operation: UPPER CUT, when a pair of Spartans hi-jacked a Covenant corvette and used a rigged slipspace drive as a makeshift bomb.

LONGSWORD
GA-TL1 INTERCEPTOR/STRIKE FIGHTER

The Longsword fighter is one of the most versatile vehicle platforms the UNSC has at its disposal and it has been at the frontlines of almost every major engagement during the Covenant War.

The Master Chief used a C709 Longsword to escape the destruction of Alpha Halo and take control of the *Ascendant Justice*.

STATISTICS

HALO: COMBAT EVOLVED
HALO 2 • HALO 3 • HALO: REACH

In the Halo: Reach multiplayer map Tempest, the debris of a crashed Longsword can be found on the beach.

MANUFACTURER: Misriah Armory
DESIGNATION: GA-TL1 Interceptor/ Strike Fighter
CREW: 1 pilot + 1 copilot + 1 navigator + 1 systems technician
LENGTH: 210.2ft (64.1m)
WIDTH: 245.9ft (75m)
PRIMARY ARMAMENT: M9109 ASW/AC 50mm MLA (2)
SECONDARY ARMAMENT: ASGM-10 (4)

FIGHTER ORIGIN

The title "GA-TL" is an abbreviation of the craft's 25th-century architects, Gov Aukland and Thomas Levesque.

Propulsion system

Cockpit

Armament and payload

VERSATILE FIGHTER

The Longsword's purpose is multi-faceted, but it can involve interception, suppression, bombing, or direct attack, and, in some instances, all of the above at once. While some Longswords, like the C709, focus on applied force in exoatmospheric engagements and are fitted with a heavy rotary cannon, others, like the C712, specialize in short-range A/X strike runs and can carry an assortment of missile and mine delivery systems. Because the GA-TL1 is such an extremely flexible vehicle, even these variations are not set in stone and can be modified on a craft-by-craft basis to fit the needs of a given mission.

LORD HOOD
FLEET ADMIRAL LORD TERRENCE HOOD

STATISTICS

HALO 2 • HALO 3

Lord Hood appears throughout Halo 2 and Halo 3, offering leadership to the UNSC in their darkest hour.

FULL NAME: Terrence Hood
SERIAL: 07960-48392-TH
BRANCH: UNSC Navy
GROUP: Home Fleet Command
RANK: Fleet Admiral
HEIGHT: 6ft 4in (192.3cm)
WEIGHT: 213lbs (96.6kg)
HOMEWORLD: Earth
DATE OF BIRTH: September 4, 2490

A member of British nobility, Lord Hood was an experienced veteran of the Navy and HIGHCOM's Security Committee and was commander of the UNSC's Home Fleet. Few are as respected as Lord Hood.

Lord Hood was a member of the UNSC Security Committee, which operated out of Sydney, Australia's HIGHCOM Facility B-6.

HUMANITY'S LEADER

Veteran of numerous military campaigns throughout his tenure, Hood gained significant renown toward the end of the Covenant War, when he single-handedly led the UNSC forces in the defense of Earth. When the Covenant first arrived at Earth in 2552, Hood launched a vigorous counter attack, keeping the enemy engaged for several weeks. A number of the Covenant forces escaped into the Forerunner Portal and Hood led the UNSC effort to wipe out the remnants of the aliens' occupation force, reclaiming safety for Earth.

INDEBTED TO THE SPARTANS

Though the details are highly classified, Hood's life was saved by Spartans more than once.

MAC

MAGNETIC ACCELERATOR CANNON

Within the UNSC, the term "MAC" refers to a heavy weapon that fires a sizeable ferric-tungsten round at supersonic speeds from the bow of a capital ship, an orbital defense platform, or driver emplacement.

"MAC" stands for "Magnetic Accelerator Cannon," although "Mass Accelerator Cannon" can also be used depending on the weapon.

Electromagnetic firing channel

PLANETARY DEFENSE

The MAC gun uses asynchronous linear induction to launch a super-dense ferric-tungsten slug at supersonic velocities. Most UNSC ships are fitted with a MAC armament as their primary firing mechanism, and orbital defense platforms are often built around an even larger weapon, called a "Super" MAC gun. Ultimately, the MAC represents humanity's best weapon against the Covenant's vast and brutal naval strength.

STATISTICS

HALO 2 • HALO 3
HALO WARS • HALO: REACH

Players get a chance to see a MAC fire up close in the Halo 2 mission "Cairo Station," as it is used in the attempt to stave off the Covenant's invasion force.

DESIGNATION: Magnetic Accelerator Cannon
AVERAGE MASS DRIVER LENGTH: 106.9ft (32.6m)
AVERAGE FRIGATE MAC LENGTH: 600.4ft (183m)
AVERAGE SUPER MAC LENGTH: 2,632ft (802.2m)
AMMUNITION: Ferric-Tungsten Slug
SHELL WEIGHT: 600 tons to 3,000 tons

Operator station

MASS DRIVER

The "Onager," or 15cm Mark/2488 1.1GJ MAC, is a powerful mass driver emplacement capable of deftly carving suborbital capital ships out of the sky.

MACHINE GUN TURRET
M247H HEAVY MACHINE GUN

AIE-486 HMG

Despite its older design, the AIE-486H fulfils the same role as other turret emplacements, particularly within the UNSC Marine Corps' primary arsenal.

Used frequently to augment fortifications and provide suppressive fire, the M247H Machine Gun is a powerful weapon that can tear through enemy lines and quickly overpower personal energy shields.

M247 GPMG

The M247 General Purpose Machine Gun is a lighter version of the M247H HMG. It fires 7.62mm rounds from a stationary position.

Defensive shield

Heavy barrel

FORTIFICATION

The M247H is an air-cooled, gas-operated, electrically fired, linkless-fed machine gun, typically mounted on a mobile tripod or a vehicle with the intention of providing infantry support. While it is most often used to fortify a defensive position and provide suppressive fire, the M247H's 12.7mm rounds can meet offensive ends when necessary, against both infantry and vehicles. Reports indicate that some soldiers have managed to remove the M247H from its mount and fire it by hand, though such scenarios seem improbable unless conducted by an augmented human.

STATISTICS

HALO 2 • HALO 3 • HALO WARS
HALO 3: ODST • HALO: REACH

Players try to keep the M247H on its tripod as long as possible, as it offers unlimited ammunition while it is fixed.

MANUFACTURER: Misriah Armory
DESIGNATION: M247H Heavy Machine Gun
AMMUNITION: 12.7mm HVE
MAGAZINE CAPACITY: 200 rounds (varies by box size)
LENGTH: 63.1in (160.2cm)
FIRING MODE : Automatic

Tripod mounting

Ammo box

MAGNUM
M6 PERSONAL DEFENSE WEAPON SYSTEM

The term "magnum" is common military shorthand for the M6 series of handguns used across all UNSC branches. The standard design uses 12.7 x 30mm caliber ammunition and is recoil-operated/magazine-fed.

Some magnums have been "up-sized" specifically for use by Spartans. Others like Kat-B320's, have even been custom tailored for use with a prosthesis.

PROMINENT FIREARM

With a wide distribution of variations, the M6 series is viewed as adaptable and versatile in almost all combat situations. As of the mid-26th century, the most popular of the series are the M6C, the M6D, and the M6G models, some of which have been customized further to use smart-linked scopes that are electronically linked to the user's armor software and heads-up display. This allows for more accurate shots at range, as well as assisting fast, perfunctory firing in quick-response situations.

Smart-linked KFA-2 scope

MISRIAH ARMORY

Customized trigger

SMART-LINK
The KFA-2 and VnSLS/V 6E suites are two of the M6 series' smart-linked sighting packages.

Magazine

STATISTICS

HALO: COMBAT EVOLVED
HALO 2 • HALO 3 • HALO WARS
HALO 3: ODST • HALO: REACH

The M6G requires evenly-paced shots to ensure that the weapon's natural recoil effect is negligible.

MANUFACTURER: Misriah Armory
DESIGNATION: M6 PDWS (Personal Defense Weapon System)
AMMUNITION: 12.7 x 30mm SAP-HE
MAGAZINE CAPACITY: 8 to 12 rounds
LENGTH (standard): 9in (22.8cm)
LENGTH (up-sized): 14in (35.5cm)
FIRING MODE: Semi-automatic

MANTIS
TYPE-27 ANTI-AIRCRAFT CANNON

STATISTICS

HALO 3
The Mantis appeared in the Halo 3 Campaign missions "The Storm" and "The Ark."

MANUFACTURER: Assembly Forges
DESIGNATION: Type-27 Anti-Aircraft Cannon
AMMUNITION: Ultra-Heavy Plasma Bolts
ENERGY CAPACITY: Unlimited
HEIGHT: 121.2ft (36.9m)
LENGTH: 196.1ft (59.8m)
FIRING MODE: Single-shot

The Mantis is a fixed, automated, heavy-grade weapon emplacement and artillery platform used by the Covenant to eliminate airborne threats with incredible accuracy and force.

Firing channel

360-degree rotational range

Marksman perch

Support strut

ACHILLES' HEEL
The T-27 Mantis' primary weakness is its heat vent which opens intermittently to prevent the weapon from overheating.

At first glance, the Mantis' firing may appear slow and cumbersome, but it can easily neutralize extremely distant targets.

MODULAR EMPLACEMENT
Like other artillery platforms, the Mantis has a girding balcony for marksmen and spotters, and an automated cooling system on its undercarriage. The main benefit of the Mantis, not shared by many other Covenant emplacements, is its modularity. The Mantis is assembled and disassembled directly on the battlefield, allowing dropships to transfer the individual parts. This makes the weapon ideal for narrow gorges and dense cityscapes.

MARK IV ARMOR
MJOLNIR POWERED ASSAULT ARMOR/MARK IV

A departure from the previous single-occupant powered armor systems, the Mark IV series was the foundation for all MJOLNIR variants to follow, and it served the Spartans for decades.

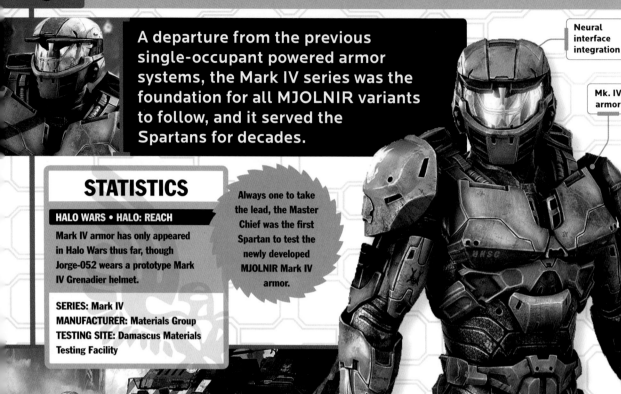

Neural interface integration

Mk. IV armor

STATISTICS

HALO WARS • HALO: REACH

Mark IV armor has only appeared in Halo Wars thus far, though Jorge-052 wears a prototype Mark IV Grenadier helmet.

SERIES: Mark IV
MANUFACTURER: Materials Group
TESTING SITE: Damascus Materials Testing Facility

Always one to take the lead, the Master Chief was the first Spartan to test the newly developed MJOLNIR Mark IV armor.

THE FIRST MJOLNIR

Mark I, Mark II, and Mark III battle armor never saw wide production due to a number of critical hurdles that could not be overcome, namely their size and their mobility-hampering power requirements. Dr. Catherine Halsey worked closely with ONI's Materials Group to develop Mark IV, a highly classified project called MJOLNIR. Although this armor technology's history was packed with incremental alterations and customizations, Mark IV remained the predominant series until November 24, 2551, when Mark V officially went active. The earliest iteration of Mark IV included a multilayer alloy, refractive coating, vacuum and temperature regulation systems, an onboard computer with neural linkage, and a reactive metal liquid crystal that enhanced speed and strength.

CHI CETI IV

Mark IV's first field test is the stuff of legend: During a naval skirmish above Chi Ceti IV, newly armored Spartans were deployed EVA. They breached the hull of a Covenant ship and detonated a nuclear weapon inside.

UNSC

MARK V ARMOR
MJOLNIR POWERED ASSAULT ARMOR/MARK V

Mk. V helmet

After the success of Mark IV, Dr. Catherine Halsey continued iterating on its design and reached Mark V; the culmination of MJOLNIR with the integration of an onboard AI construct.

Mark V [B], a secretly produced alternate version to Mark V, was first used by SPARTAN-III personnel.

STATISTICS

HALO: COMBAT EVOLVED • HALO 3 HALO: REACH

Mark V first appeared in Halo: Combat Evolved, worn by the Master Chief, though a precursor of this design is used by Noble Team in Halo: Reach.

SERIES: Mark V
MANUFACTURER: Materials Group
TESTING SITE: Damascus Materials Testing Facility

Mk. V —undersuit mesh

PERSONAL SHIELDS

Energy shielding was a key feature of Mark V, although other Spartan squads had field-tested prototypes of this technology as early as 2531.

UPGRADED ARMOR

The MJOLNIR Mark V platform provided the foundation for numerous armor variants. One of the notable features of Mark V is its energy shielding technology, developed from reverse-engineered Covenant matériel. While Mark V officially entered service on November 24, 2551, it wasn't until nearly a year later, on August 29, 2552, that it reached its zenith through the integration of a UNSC Artificial Intelligence for Operation: RED FLAG. Master Chief Petty Officer John-117 was the first Spartan to wear this finalized version of the armor, which integrated the AI known as Cortana by way of an upgraded neural interface.

MARK VI ARMOR
MJOLNIR POWERED ASSAULT ARMOR/MARK VI

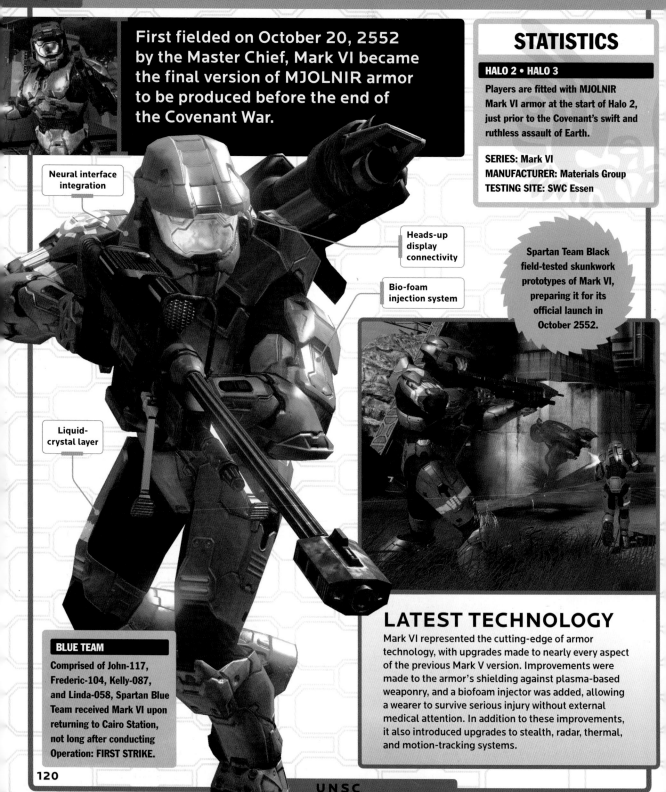

First fielded on October 20, 2552 by the Master Chief, Mark VI became the final version of MJOLNIR armor to be produced before the end of the Covenant War.

STATISTICS

HALO 2 • HALO 3

Players are fitted with MJOLNIR Mark VI armor at the start of Halo 2, just prior to the Covenant's swift and ruthless assault of Earth.

SERIES: Mark VI
MANUFACTURER: Materials Group
TESTING SITE: SWC Essen

Neural interface integration

Heads-up display connectivity

Bio-foam injection system

Spartan Team Black field-tested skunkwork prototypes of Mark VI, preparing it for its official launch in October 2552.

Liquid-crystal layer

BLUE TEAM

Comprised of John-117, Frederic-104, Kelly-087, and Linda-058, Spartan Blue Team received Mark VI upon returning to Cairo Station, not long after conducting Operation: FIRST STRIKE.

LATEST TECHNOLOGY

Mark VI represented the cutting-edge of armor technology, with upgrades made to nearly every aspect of the previous Mark V version. Improvements were made to the armor's shielding against plasma-based weaponry, and a biofoam injector was added, allowing a wearer to survive serious injury without external medical attention. In addition to these improvements, it also introduced upgrades to stealth, radar, thermal, and motion-tracking systems.

STATISTICS

HALO: COMBAT EVOLVED
HALO 2 • HALO 3

The Master Chief is the central figure of the Halo story, but he has only appeared in three of the Halo games.

FULL NAME: John-117
SERVICE NUMBER: S-117
BRANCH: UNSC Navy
GROUP: Naval Special Weapons, SPARTAN-II
RANK: Master Chief Petty Officer
HEIGHT: 7ft 2in (218cm)
WEIGHT: 395lbs (179kg)
HOMEWORLD: Eridanus II
DATE OF BIRTH: [CLASSIFIED]

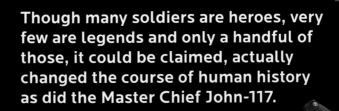

Though many soldiers are heroes, very few are legends and only a handful of those, it could be claimed, actually changed the course of human history as did the Master Chief John-117.

Mk. VI armor

LEGENDARY SPARTAN

Abducted at the age of six, John was conscripted into the SPARTAN-II project, trained, and augmented to be a super-soldier without equal. For nearly three decades, he fought against the Covenant, and was instrumental in discovering Halo and the secrets of the Forerunners. After witnessing the High Prophet of Truth excavate the ancient Forerunner artifact below the Earth's surface, the Master Chief pursued the Covenant to the Ark, where he not only ended their reign of terror, but stopped both the Flood and the threat of the Halo Array.

Titanium alloy shell

The Chief was paired with the powerful UNSC AI Cortana in late 2552; this was done in preparation for Operation: RED FLAG.

STATUS: UNKNOWN

After the Ark's destruction, the Master Chief and Cortana lost contact with the UNSC. Their current status remains unknown.

Battle-worn plating

MAULER
TYPE-52 PISTOL

The Brute Mauler is a one-handed, gas-operated trench gun functionally similar to a human shotgun. It fires superheated, crudely shaped 7.9mm metal bolts and is primarily designed for close-quarters combat.

The Mauler is commonly used by Brute Stalkers and was seen frequently during the battle on the Forerunner Ark.

Chamber **Barrel**

BATTLE OF GBRAAKON

The Mauler first saw use during a violent conflict in the Gbraakon territory on Doisac, shortly after the Brutes' global war.

Grip

Guard blade

STATISTICS

HALO 3 • HALO 3: ODST

Halo 3 and Halo 3: ODST are the only games to feature the Brutes' Mauler.

MANUFACTURER: Sacred Promissory
DESIGNATION: Type-52 Pistol
AMMUNITION: 7.9mm Bolts
MAGAZINE CAPACITY: 5 Shots
LENGTH: 20.8in (52.7cm)
FIRING MODE: Semi-automatic

CRUDE WEAPONRY

The Mauler's crude yet simple design allows for resiliency in the field, but its poor barrel choke makes it largely inaccurate outside of close-quarters combat. Although it doesn't possess the overall stopping power of the UNSC's M45 or M90 shotguns, it can easily hold its own against shielded enemies. Additionally, like other Brute weapons, the Mauler brandishes a razor-sharp guard blade at the bottom of its grip, which can easily puncture an enemy's armor and cause tremendous physical harm.

STATISTICS

HALO 3: ODST

In the Halo 3: ODST mission "Kizingo Boulevard," players take on the role of Mickey as he heads to the ONI building.

FULL NAME: Michael Crespo
SERVICE NUMBER: 51033-15973-MC
BRANCH: UNSC Marine Corps
GROUP: Naval Special Weapons, Orbital Drop Shock Troopers
RANK: Private First Class
HEIGHT: 6ft (184cm)
WEIGHT: 187.3lbs (85kg)
HOMEWORLD: Luna
DATE OF BIRTH: October 20, 2530

Over the short time that Mickey Crespo has served in the UNSC Marine Corps, he has proven himself to be not only a skilled pilot and seasoned demolitions expert, but a dedicated member of the ODST.

M41 Rocket Launcher

Demolitions gear

EXPERTISE IN THE FIELD

After enlisting in 2548, Michael "Mickey" Crespo served as a Pelican crew chief and a demolitions specialist, and eventually joined the ODST. On October 20, 2552, he and his squad were ordered to secure classified data from the Covenant in the besieged city of New Mombasa. There, he assisted with the demolition of the ONI Alpha Site, using a stolen Covenant Phantom to secure both his team and the data as they escaped the devastated city.

URBAN WARFARE

During the Covenant's occupation of New Mombasa, Mickey used a Scorpion tank to forge his way to ONI's Alpha Site.

ODST/UA PPE

MIDSHIP
MULTIPLAYER MAP

Midship's fixed symmetry, clean lines of sight, and bowl-like shape are largely unmatched in Halo multiplayer, turning the arena-style map into a competitive haven for both free-for-all and team gametypes.

STATISTICS

HALO 2 • HALO 3

While free-for-all gametypes played exceptionally well on Midship, the map's biggest successes were in team-based gametypes, particularly Slayer, Capture the Flag, and Assault.

ENVIRONMENT: Covenant cruiser deck
RELEVANCE: *Pious Inquisitor* viewing deck
LAYOUT: Symmetrical arena-style
PLAYER COUNT: 2 to 8
KEY WEAPONS: Energy Sword, Shotgun

LOCATIONS OVER TIME

Set aboard the battlecruiser *Pious Inquisitor,* Midship and Heretic are the same location at different times. Midship takes place just before the Covenant's invasion of Earth; while Heretic occurs as rebel Elites pursue a Flood-infected cruiser back to Earth.

Victory on Midship often meant acquiring the Energy Sword or Shotgun, though skilled players could use the Battle Rifle to control the map as well.

COVENANT ARENA

Small, open, and yet replete with cover, Halo 2's Midship became the model for competitive multiplayer environments in Halo for years after it was released. The Covenant cruiser deck consists of two main levels: Below are a pair of nearly identical rooms with connecting walkways and corridors encircling a Shotgun-occupied central floor. Above sits the second level of each aforementioned room and a single lone platform that holds the elegant but deadly Energy Sword.

COVENANT

When removed from its emplacement, the Missile Pod can only fire eight missiles before requiring more ammunition.

The Missile Pod is a weapon emplacement launcher unit (LAU) that fires self-guided missiles (SGM) from a stationary position. Its ordnance is capable of seeking and tracking targets for long distances.

Forward grip

Ammunition housing

STATISTICS

HALO 3 • HALO 3: ODST

To achieve the best accuracy with the Missile Pod, the player should ensure it's locked onto its target before firing.

MANUFACTURER: Ushuaia Armory
SERIES: Launcher Unit-65D/
Self-Guided Missiles-151
AMMUNITION: Automatic Self-Guided Missiles-4
MAGAZINE CAPACITY: 8 missiles
LENGTH: 79.7in (202.4cm)
FIRING MODE: Semi-automatic

Rear grip

HEAVY EMPLACEMENT

When mounted in a fixed emplacement, the Missile Pod can fire its ASGM-4 missiles for extended periods of time thanks to large magazines in the base of the emplacement. Missiles are at first propelled by the pod before initiating their automated self-propulsion guidance system. Some have reported seeing troops remove the pod from its emplacement to use it in a mobile position, but such reports are inconclusive.

Stationary mount

MISSILE CLASSIFICATION

ASGM-10 missiles are in the same series as the lower-grade, self-guided ASGM-4s. They are used on aircraft like GA-TL1 Longsword Interceptors.

MONGOOSE
M274 ULTRA-LIGHT ALL-TERRAIN VEHICLE

The Mongoose is an unarmed **UNSC** transport which offers high speed and dexterity. With a skilled driver and a passenger who knows how to handle heavy artillery while on the move, this nimble vehicle can be a powerful asset.

STATISTICS

HALO 3 • HALO 3: ODST
HALO: REACH

The Mongoose is used in Halo multiplayer for quick flag grabs or bomb plants in objective-based gametypes.

MANUFACTURER: AMG Transport Dynamics
DESIGNATION: M274 Ultra-Light All-Terrain Vehicle
CREW: 1 driver + 1 passenger
LENGTH: 10.5ft (3.2m)
WIDTH: 6.1ft (1.8m)

SWIFT TRANSPORTATION

Manufactured by AMG Transport Dynamics, the M274 represents one of the most agile and swift vehicles the UNSC has on the ground in the war against the Covenant. Designed for one operator and the choice of a passenger or cargo, the Mongoose was built to provide quick troop conveyance across short distances. While it may not seem imposing to enemy infantry, since it lacks protection and offensive weaponry, the Mongoose is still capable of being a formidable military tool.

Cargo rack

Side-view mirror

Speed, maneuverability, and its small size all make the M247 an excellent agent for hit-and-run combat maneuvers.

Hydrogen-injected ICE

ATV suspension system

STATISTICS

HALO: REACH

Going from Halo 3: ODST to Halo: Reach, the Needle Rifle came to replace the Covenant Carbine for many players.

MANUFACTURER: Sacred Promissory
DESIGNATION: Type-31 Rifle
AMMUNITION: Crystalline Shards
MAGAZINE CAPACITY: 21 shards
LENGTH: 49.9in (126.7cm)
FIRING MODE: Automatic, semi-automatic

Designed as a mid-range weapon, the Needle Rifle combines the deadly explosive effect of a Needler with the fierce accuracy of the Covenant Carbine. This rifle is typically used by Elites and Jackal marksmen.

Optics system

Crystalline shard

Barrel

Unlike the T-33 Needler, the T-31 Rifle's needles are not designed to home in on a target and therefore must be fired like a marksman rifle.

Grip

MARKSMAN RIFLE

Much like the Needler, the Type-31 Rifle uses a crystalline latticework of ammunition that is exposed on the weapon's stock. As the gun is fired, the crystalline shards snap off into individual charged projectiles, which are launched linearly at the target. The main difference between the Needle Rifle and the smaller Needler is that the former can fire both automatically and semi-automatically, and it has an electronic sighting system for mid-range combat. In many respects, the Needle Rifle is also very similar to the Covenant's T-51 Carbine, the key difference here being ammunition: While the Needle Rifle's ammunition lacks the radioactive material used by the carbine, three shots from it planted into the flesh of an unshielded enemy will cause an immediate and violent explosion.

NEEDLER
TYPE-33 GUIDED MUNITIONS LAUNCHER

The elaborate nature of the Needler's design is also an aspect of its functionality, which revolves around the firing of individual, crystalline shards which explode after impaling an enemy.

STATISTICS

HALO: COMBAT EVOLVED
HALO 2 • HALO 3 • HALO WARS
HALO 3: ODST • HALO: REACH

In Halo 2, the Needler can be dual-wielded, allowing players to fire one in each hand.

MANUFACTURER: Sacred Promissory
DESIGNATION: Type-33 Guided Munitions Launcher
AMMUNITION: Crystalline Shards
MAGAZINE CAPACITY: 24 shards (varies)
   LENGTH: 29.3in (74.3cm)
   FIRING MODE: Automatic

SCARED PROMISSORY

The Sacred Promissory is a lower district munitions factory responsible for most needle-based weaponry and, later, all Brute-designed matériel.

The raw material used as the source of the Needler's crystalline shard is mined from Suban, one of Sanghelios' two moons.

Exposed shard

Grip

Under-channel brace

Hand guard

EXPLOSIVE WEAPON

The operation of the Needler is based chiefly on its ammo: a series of individual crystalline latticework needles lodged in the weapon's cowling. The Needler breaks these needles, charges their chemical mixture, and fires them off in a fluid, automatic fashion. The shards launch toward a targeted heat signature, tracking and impaling it. Upon entering a target, the shard becomes chemically reactive and detonates. If more than one shard makes contact, as is typically the case, they detonate simultaneously— a chain reaction that is almost always lethal.

NEW MOMBASA

EAST AFRICAN PROTECTORATE, EARTH

THE SUPERINTENDENT

Like Earth's other tether cities, New Mombasa was managed by an urban infrastructure AI.

Prior to the Covenant's invasion, New Mombasa was one of the most renowned and majestic cities on Earth. Tragically, the aliens destroyed it in their relentless search for the Forerunners' Ark installation.

GROUND ZERO

New Mombasa represented the heart and soul of the East African Protectorate. Home to the New Mombasa Orbital Elevator as well as a major site for ONI, the city held significant value to the UNSC and all humanity. On October 20, 2552, the Covenant arrived at Earth and mysteriously focused their efforts solely on this city. It was only later, as New Mombasa was glassed by a Covenant fleet, that an ancient artifact was revealed below its surface. This machine would hold the key to humanity's survival and victory against the Covenant.

STATISTICS

HALO 2 • HALO 3: ODST

The entirety of Halo 3: ODST is played in New Mombasa, shortly after the *Solemn Penance* slipped away, severely battering the city in the process.

PLANET: Earth
COUNTRY: Republic of Kenya, East African Protectorate
GOVERNMENT SITES: NMPD Headquarters, ONI Alpha Site, Data Center
COMMERCIAL SITES: New Mombasa Space Tether, Uplift Nature Reserve

In 2302, New Mombasa was selected as Earth's first city to have a space tether.

Vyrant Telecom tower

Uplift Reserve

Liwitoni district

NOBLE SIX
LIEUTENANT S-B312, SPARTAN-III

Very little information exists about S-B312, a SPARTAN-III culled from the rank and file of Beta Company. What is known is that he showed exemplary skill in both ground-based and orbital missions.

Mk. V [B] variant

MA37 Assault Rifle

M6G Magnum

STATISTICS

HALO: REACH

Noble Six is the avatar through which players experience Halo: Reach's Campaign. The Spartan's gender and armor can be determined by the player.

FULL NAME: [CLASSIFIED]
SERVICE NUMBER: S-B312
BRANCH: UNSC Army
GROUP: Special Warfare, Group Three
RANK: Lieutenant
HEIGHT: 6ft 9in (205.7cm)
WEIGHT: 239.4lbs (108.6kg)
HOMEWORLD: [CLASSIFIED]
DATE OF BIRTH: [CLASSIFIED]
DATE OF DEATH: August 30, 2552

PROVING HIMSELF

Spartan-B312 was at first not welcomed by Noble Team due to their feelings for the previous Noble Six who was recently KIA. However, his impressive performance during the fight for Reach dramatically changed the team's opinion of him.

Alone at the end, and with Covenant forces encroaching, Noble Six fought to the death on the debris-strewn fields of Aszod.

LONE WOLF

The bulk of this super-soldier's career was spent in lone wolf operations, outside of a standard team element until 2552, when he was requisitioned to the planet Reach and assigned to Noble Team. Now known as Noble Six, he fought alongside the other members of Noble. He was later selected for the special mission of delivering the AI known as Cortana to the UNSC *Pillar of Autumn*. While he succeeded in this objective, Six fell during the ensuing battle against an insurmountable and merciless Covenant force.

ODST

Most ODST teams have 10 to 14 operators, each of which plays a specific role, though all are trained for any combat situation.

ODST, or Orbital Drop Shock Troopers, are the UNSC Marine Corps' most elite personnel. They are known for their combat specialization and fearless deployment, being fired down toward a planet's surface from space.

UA/Bullfrog BDU

40mm Grenades

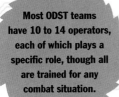

STATISTICS

HALO 2 • HALO 3 • HALO WARS HALO 3: ODST • HALO: REACH

For the first time in Halo, players were given the opportunity to jump into the boots of an ODST in Halo 3: ODST.

BRANCH: UNSC Marine Corps
OPERATIONAL AUTHORITY: Naval Special Weapons
FUNCTION: Deep ground surveillance (DGS), direct action (DA), unconventional warfare, counter-terrorism operations, counter-contraband operations, special equipment recovery/capture

FEET FIRST INTO HELL

Orbital Drop Shock Troopers perform highly specialized, small-scale operations, from surveillance and reconnaissance within enemy territory to counter-terrorism and unconventional warfare. They are considered to be the UNSC Marine Corps' best-trained and most resilient soldiers, and are known for their method of deployment in which they are individually launched to a planet's surface from space.

ORBITAL DEPLOYMENT

The SOEIV (Single Occupant Exoatmospheric Insertion Vehicle), or drop pod, allows ODST to be orbitally deployed deep into the heart of enemy territory.

ONI ALPHA SITE
OFFICE OF NAVAL INTELLIGENCE, ALPHA SITE

The Office of Naval Intelligence's Alpha Site had all of the exterior trappings of a standard ONI administration building. Buried deep below, however, lay a number of secrets, some which the Covenant were after.

HALO 3: ODST

In the Halo 3: ODST missions "ONI Alpha Site" and "Data Hive," players can explore this massive complex.

DESIGNATION: Office of Naval Intelligence, Alpha Site
LOCATION: New Mombasa, Earth
PRIMARY PURPOSE: Official EAP HQ for the Office of Naval Intelligence
CONFIDENTIAL PURPOSE: Data aggregator for proximal alien artifact

CRITICAL SITE

The Office of Naval Intelligence's Alpha Site, located in the southern-most portion of New Mombasa, was designed to be a grand, public-facing complex with a large courtyard and a towering onyx façade. Underneath this majestic structure, however, was something much less public. Buried deep below Alpha Site was a massive data complex housing New Mombasa's superintendant AI construct, from where all of the city's urban infrastructural tasks were managed. When the UNSC learned that the Covenant were after the information stored below ONI's building, they destroyed the site and extracted the data.

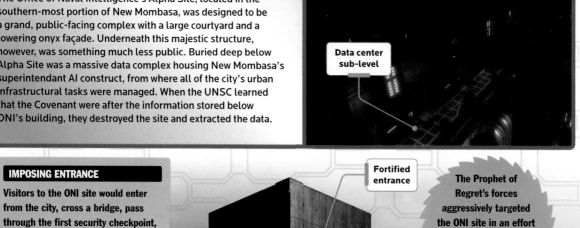

Data center sub-level

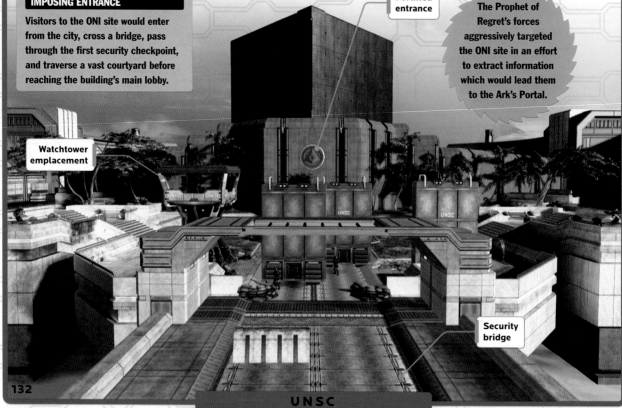

IMPOSING ENTRANCE

Visitors to the ONI site would enter from the city, cross a bridge, pass through the first security checkpoint, and traverse a vast courtyard before reaching the building's main lobby.

Fortified entrance

The Prophet of Regret's forces aggressively targeted the ONI site in an effort to extract information which would lead them to the Ark's Portal.

Watchtower emplacement

Security bridge

OPERATOR ARMOR

MJOLNIR POWERED ASSAULT ARMOR—OPERATOR

Operator armor is a variation of MJOLNIR armor developed specifically for Spartans working within Beta-5 Division's own Asymmetrical Action Group (AAG).

B5D-O/ Optics Suite

Mk. V—AAG modified

UNCONVENTIONAL WARFARE

Beta-5 Division's Asymmetrical Action Group (AAG) was the ONI's cross-branch effort to disarm, disrupt, and dissolve Covenant activities late into the war. AAG originally began with veterans of unconventional warfare, but as time passed it came to include Spartans. While these specific "operators" used their own standard armor, B5D worked with Chalybs Defense Solutions to create a variant of MJOLNIR that exclusively benefitted AAG operators in the field. The armor provided detailed, on-the-fly intel through transmissions that could circumvent most Covenant security networks.

MC5 Tactical Dock

PARTICLE BEAM RIFLE
TYPE-50 SNIPER RIFLE SYSTEM

The Particle Beam Rifle is believed to ionize hydrogen gas, using a linear accelerator to fire a devastating beam of charged particles; something far beyond humanity's conventional infantry combat technology.

STATISTICS

HALO 2 • HALO 3 • HALO 3: ODST

Using the Beam Rifle's incredible accuracy to land clean headshots is the most effective use of the weapon.

MANUFACTURER: Iruiru Armory
DESIGNATION: Type-50 Sniper Rifle System
AMMUNITION: Ionized Hydrogen
ENERGY CAPACITY: 10 units
LENGTH: 63.1in (160.3cm)
FIRING MODE: Semi-automatic

Optics integration

Coil set

Accelerator channel

Grip

SNIPER OPTICS

Despite their excellent natural optical acuity, Jackals often employ the use of customized sighting hardware that is directly integrated with the T-50 SRS.

For the T-50 SRS, the coil set is used to collect and charge particles prior to their hyper-acceleration along the firing channel.

MARKSMAN'S WEAPON

Its exact origin is shrouded in mystery, but the Type-50 Sniper Rifle System is an example of the Covenant's proficient understanding of linear particle acceleration. The weapon was developed in Iruiru, Yermo of Sanghelios, the Elites' homeworld, though its design appears to have been refined and iterated upon over time. As a ranged combat weapon, it matches and many times exceeds the performance of the UNSC's SRS99 series of sniper rifles, being lighter in weight and having a faster overall muzzle velocity.

PELICAN

D77-TC PELICAN DROPSHIP

Many later Pelicans sport a rear-facing heavy machine gun mounted at the bay door.

The Pelican is the UNSC's primary method of troop transportation and deployment. It is capable of operating both in and out of atmosphere, as well as providing direct fire against enemy contacts when needed.

Cockpit

Anvil-II Missile Pod

STATISTICS

**HALO: COMBAT EVOLVED
HALO 2 • HALO 3 • HALO WARS
HALO 3: ODST • HALO: REACH**

In Halo 3: ODST, players see their first civilian variant of the Pelican dropship in the D77C-NMPD.

MANUFACTURER: Misriah Armory
DESIGNATION: D77-TC Pelican Dropship
CREW: 3 crew + 10 passengers
LENGTH: 102.3ft (31.2m)
WIDTH: 83.7ft (25.5m)
PRIMARY ARMAMENT: HE Anvil-II Air-to-Surface Missile Launchers (2)
SECONDARY ARMAMENT: M370 Autocannon "Chin Gun"

M370 Autocannon

NMPD PELICAN

Pelicans come in a variety of configurations, all depending on the specific needs of the client.

DEPENDABLE DEPLOYMENT

The D77-TC Pelican dropship is one of the most common and well-known UNSC vehicles. In addition to having an M370 autocannon, nearly all Pelicans are equipped with a pair of HE Anvil-II Air-to-Surface Missile Launchers, which can effectively engage most enemy counterparts. The dropship's ability to swiftly heft troops and vehicles from one site to another, provide firing support from the air, or simply convey matériel to and from ships in space, make the Pelican an important and necessary part of 26th-century warfare.

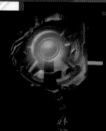

For many millennia, 2401 Penitent Tangent operated as the Monitor of Delta Halo with efficiency and exactitude. Not long before the conflict on Halo, something went awry and he became a victim of the Flood.

STATISTICS

HALO 2

After the Halo 2 mission "Sacred Icon," the player sees Penitent Tangent for the first time, compromised and in the clutches of the Gravemind.

FULL NAME: 2401 Penitent Tangent (05-2401)
ORIGIN: Forerunner
CLASS: Artificial Intelligence
ROLE: Monitor
AGE: 100,000 years (approx)
LOCATION: Installation 05 (Delta Halo)
LENGTH: 22.9in (58.2cm)
WIDTH: 19.9in (50.6cm)

DERELICTION OR DEPOSITION?

Early reports indicated that Tangent was derelict in his duties and contributed to the Flood's outbreak and his own capture. This seems unlikely, however, as he continued, for some time, to advocate the firing of Delta Halo.

It is believed that Tangent was on Delta Halo when the Elites cauterized the Flood infection. His current status remains unknown.

CAPTIVE OF THE FLOOD

Little is known about 2401 Penitent Tangent apart from the fact that he was an AI construct who served as the Monitor for Installation 05 and played a serious role in the most recent Flood outbreak. Several hundred years ago, a mysterious breach in Delta Halo's security contributed to a catastrophic containment failure. With the parasite released, it soon formed a Gravemind and then waited centuries, ultimately setting a trap for any unsuspecting visitor that might stumble upon the site. Tangent was last seen in the possession of the Gravemind, which adds a measure of intrigue to the events preceding the Flood parasite's galactic reemergence.

PHANTOM
TYPE-52 TROOP CARRIER

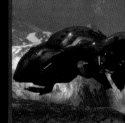

STATISTICS

**HALO 2 • HALO 3 • HALO 3: ODST
HALO: REACH**

In the Halo: Reach mission "New Alexandria," a cleverly crafted Easter egg allows players to fly a Phantom or Pelican throughout the city.

MANUFACTURER: Assembly Forges
DESIGNATION: Type-52 Troop Carrier
CREW: 1 pilot + 1 weapon officer + 2 gunners + 30 passengers (varies)
LENGTH: 109.6ft (33.4m)
WIDTH: 66.8ft (20.4m)
PRIMARY ARMAMENT:
Heavy Plasma Cannon
SECONDARY ARMAMENT:
Type-52 Directed Energy Support Weapon (2)

The Phantom dropship offers a quick, well-armed (and armored) delivery of a relatively large number of Covenant troops in both atmospheric and exoatmospheric conditions.

Armored hull

The T-52's lateral plasma cannons can be removed from their tripods and carried into battle.

T-52 DESW

Heavy Plasma Cannon

Pilot cockpit

KEY VULNERABILITY

The Phantom's twin turbines expose its propulsion system, which is connected to its power supply. This vulnerability can quickly bring the T-52 dropship down.

VERSATILE DROPSHIP

The Type-52 Troop Carrier, or Phantom, is easily the most practical of the Covenant dropships, offering a relatively small, streamlined design alongside impressive speed and the ability to convey up to 30 passengers from its side bay doors or from its ventral gravity lift. Most versions have a single heavy plasma cannon mounted underneath the prow with a pair of medium plasma cannons guarding both bay doors, though there are a variety of other configurations.

PILLAR OF AUTUMN

UNSC PILLAR OF AUTUMN C-709

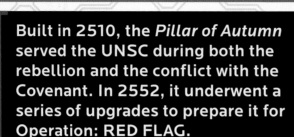

Built in 2510, the *Pillar of Autumn* served the UNSC during both the rebellion and the conflict with the Covenant. In 2552, it underwent a series of upgrades to prepare it for Operation: RED FLAG.

STATISTICS

HALO: COMBAT EVOLVED
HALO 2 • HALO: REACH

In the final mission of Halo: Combat Evolved, players must escape the *Pillar of Autumn* before its reactors detonate.

REGISTRY: C-709
CLASS: *Halcyon*-class Light Cruiser
COMMANDING OFFICER: Jacob Keyes
LENGTH: 3,841ft (1,171m)
BEAM: 1,156ft (352m)
PRIMARY ARMAMENT:
Magnetic Accelerator Cannon
SECONDARY ARMAMENT:
Missile Delivery System
TERTIARY ARMAMENT:
Point Defense System

Titanium-A battleplate

At first, *Autumn*'s design was viewed as overmassed and cost prohibitive. Decades later it would prove essential for the needs of RED FLAG.

Point Defense System

Command deck

RESURRECTED FOR WAR

Formidable and heavily armed, the UNSC *Pillar of Autumn* was extensively upgraded for Operation: RED FLAG, a classified mission that intended to send it and its crew deep into Covenant-controlled space. RED FLAG's goal was the capture of a Covenant Prophet, but when the aliens suddenly arrived at Reach, the *Autumn* narrowly evaded their assault by escaping into the unknown of slipspace. Eventually they arrived at Installation 04, where the UNSC came face to face with the threat of both Halo and the Flood. The Master Chief used the *Autumn*'s fusion reactors to destroy Halo, along with the local Flood and Covenant forces.

PILOT ARMOR
MJOLNIR POWERED ASSAULT ARMOR—PILOT

STATISTICS

HALO: REACH

Players can purchase Pilot armor in Halo: Reach for 90,000 credits after acquiring the rank of Commander.

SERIES: Mark IV/Mark V
MANUFACTURER: Chalybs Defense Solutions
TESTING SITE: Chalybs Testing Preserve

Most Spartan units operate within the UNSC Navy and Army. However, a select few serve in the UNSC's Air Force and they are typically clad in the modified MJOLNIR variant dubbed "Pilot."

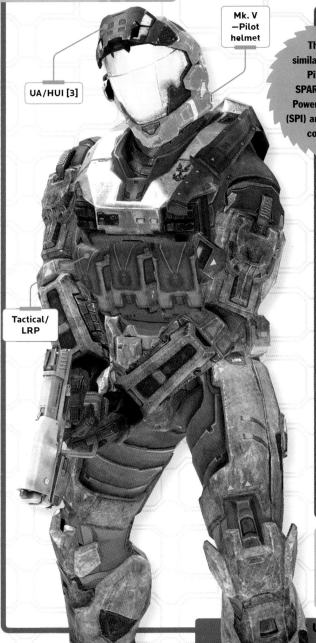

UA/HUI [3]

Mk. V —Pilot helmet

The physical similarities between Pilot and the SPARTAN-III Semi-Powered Infiltration (SPI) armor are strictly coincidental.

Tactical/ LRP

AIR FORCE ARMOR

The Pilot armor variant was designed exclusively for Spartan pilots and combat controllers and is intended for engagements both in and out of atmosphere. The armor's main benefits are the user's increased field of vision and a collection of air/space operational and tactical software integrated directly onto the armor's heads-up display.

JOINT DEVELOPMENT

Chalybs worked closely with the Materials Group based out of Ganymede, the team developing MJOLNIR's EVA variant. This collaboration is evident in the armor's hardware architecture.

UNSC

PLASMA CANNON
TYPE-52 DIRECTED ENERGY SUPPORT WEAPON

STATISTICS

**HALO 3 • HALO 3: ODST
HALO: REACH**

When dismounting a support weapon like the Plasma Cannon, players will switch to third-person and move more slowly while carrying it.

MANUFACTURER: Assembly Forges
DESIGNATION: Type-52 Directed Energy Support Weapon
AMMUNITION: Superheated Plasma
ENERGY CAPACITY: 200 units (dismounted)
LENGTH: 62.3in (158.3cm)
FIRING MODE: Automatic

The Plasma Cannon is a tripod-mounted energy turret that fires superheated bursts of plasma. It typically serves as a stationary emplacement for both direct and suppressive fire.

The energy shield plating and the modular cooling system are two examples of improvements of the T-52 over earlier versions.

Shielding

Cooling unit

EARLIER ITERATIONS
The T-42 cannon has similar operation systems, but was phased out due to the better overall performance of the T-52.

Circuit emitter

SUPPORT EMPLACEMENT

Like most turret emplacements, the Plasma Cannon was designed to provide defensive positions with both direct and suppressive fire, while allowing the ease of transportability—something the larger T-26 Shade is incapable of. The weapon is particularly useful against energy-shielded enemies, since its high muzzle velocity can overwhelm a target's shielding systems quickly. The Plasma Cannon can also be removed and carried into battle without the use of a mounting system, though this is rarely witnessed, due to the size and weight of the weapon.

PLASMA GRENADE
TYPE-1 ANTIPERSONNEL GRENADE

Due to its effective performance, reliability, and relatively easy transportability, the Plasma Grenade has seen very few improvements.

The Plasma Grenade is the Covenant's oft used antipersonnel explosive. It exploits the ability of the Covenant's shaped plasma to adhere to moving objects or those emitting distinguishable heat signatures.

Grenade detonation

STATISTICS

HALO: COMBAT EVOLVED
HALO 2 • HALO 3 • HALO WARS
HALO 3: ODST • HALO: REACH

Affectionately referred to as the "Sticky Grenade," the Plasma Grenade appears in every Halo game.

MANUFACTURER: Iruiru Armory
DESIGNATION: Type-1 Antipersonnel Grenade
FILLER: Latent Plasma
DIAMETER: 5.75in (14.6cm)
KILLING RADIUS: 12.9ft (3.9m)
CASUALTY RADIUS: 42.3ft (12.9m)

Priming button

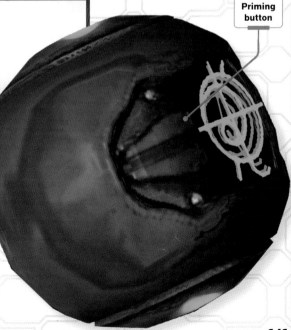

RESOURCEFUL DESIGN

The Type-1 Antipersonnel Grenade or Plasma Grenade is a spherical, time-detonated explosive, not very different from the conventional antipersonnel grenades of the UNSC. Its detonation is triggered by pressing a button on its shell that primes the grenade and engulfs it in a bloom of plasma energy. Once the button is released, the grenade will detonate based on the fuse settings that have been previously applied. During the fuse's countdown, the plasma can bond to any moving object, typically those of a certain size and carrying a prominent heat signature. Once the fuse has run its course, the grenade will detonate.

BOREN'S SYNDROME

It has been theorized that prolonged exposure to the energy yielded by plasma grenades can cause Boren's Syndrome in humans; a neural pathway disorder.

PLASMA LAUNCHER
TYPE-52 GUIDED MUNITIONS LAUNCHER/EXPLOSIVE

The Plasma Launcher is a shoulder-mounted anti-personnel/anti-matériel weapon capable of firing up to four guided plasma bolts, which detonate once they've adhered to the target.

Targeting sensor

Launching chamber

Rear grip

TACTICAL USES

The T-52 GML/E can fire bolts semi-automatically, which is incredibly effective when properly used against infantry.

Fore grip

The Plasma Launcher is based on the same Covenant technology used on almost all of their self-guided munitions.

POWERFUL ORDNANCE

The Plasma Launcher is a versatile guided munitions weapon which, in the hands of a well-trained combatant, can be incredibly deadly. The launcher operates by generating up to four superheated plasma bolts simultaneously before tuning them to actively track a target selected by the weapon's operator. Due to the Plasma Launcher's 2.5x zoom capability, targeting can be done with great accuracy over relatively large distances. Once the operator has fired the weapon, the four bolts will actively pursue the target, adhering to it before detonating violently.

PLASMA PISTOL
TYPE-25 DIRECTED ENERGY PISTOL

ORIGINAL DESIGN

The Plasma Pistol's success in the field has meant very few changes in its design since the earliest models first entered production.

The Plasma Pistol is a single-handed weapon found in most Covenant troop deployments. This pervasiveness is likely due to its exceptional rate of fire and its efficiency against energy shielding.

Charging poles

Rear grip

Fore grip

STATISTICS

HALO: COMBAT EVOLVED
HALO 2 • HALO 3 • HALO WARS
HALO 3: ODST • HALO: REACH

Halo 3 introduced the Plasma Pistol's ability to temporarily stun and disable enemy vehicles.

MANUFACTURER: Iruiru Armory
DESIGNATION: Type-25 Directed Energy Pistol
AMMUNITION: Charged Plasma Bursts
ENERGY CAPACITY: 100 units
LENGTH: 14.5in (37cm)
FIRING MODE: Semi-automatic

The Iruiru Armory, located on Yermo's western tombolo clusters, manufactures the Plasma Pistol.

COVENANT FIREARM

In its standard, semi-automatic function, the Plasma Pistol is ideal for close combat, as it provides a high rate of fire and reasonable accuracy over short distances. If the trigger is held down, the front charging poles generate a scaled burst—referred to as "overcharging" the weapon. When released, the scaled burst will emit, briefly tracking a targeted object. This causes increased damage but it can also knock out energy capacitors in equipment, armor, and vehicles, stopping enemy transports in their tracks.

PLASMA REPEATER
TYPE-51 DIRECTED ENERGY RIFLE/IMPROVED

While the Plasma Repeater looks and functions similarly to the standard Plasma Rifle, key improvements have made it not only more powerful, but also more reliable in the field.

Unlike the T-25, the T-51 never overheats. It automatically slows the rate of fire, reminding the user to manually vent the rifle's shroud.

UPGRADED RIFLE

Relatively new to the battlefield, the Type-51 Directed Energy Rifle/Improved, or Plasma Repeater, is believed to be either an improvement on the existing Plasma Rifle, or, more likely, a variant exclusive to a number of Covenant detachments. Whatever the case, the weapon's basic operation is similar to most directed-energy arms that the Covenant employ, although it has several advantages over other weapons of this type. Not only does it have a faster rate of fire and a heavier bolt than the standard Plasma Rifle, but it also allows the user the ability to manually vent the rifle's residual heat.

Shroud vent

Trigger

Charging poles

Circuit emitter

STATISTICS

HALO: REACH

Like other Covenant energy weapons, the Plasma Repeater is incredibly effective against shielded opponents.

MANUFACTURER: Iruiru Armory
DESIGNATION: Type-51 Directed Energy Rifle/Improved
AMMUNITION: Superheated Plasma
ENERGY CAPACITY: 100 units
LENGTH: 38.3in (97.4cm)
FIRING MODE: Automatic

AFFORDABILITY

The prominence of Covenant energy weapons is directly connected to the affordability of their ammunition.

STATISTICS

PLASMA RIFLE
TYPE-25 DIRECTED ENERGY RIFLE

HALO: COMBAT EVOLVED
HALO 2 • HALO 3 • HALO WARS
HALO 3: ODST • HALO: REACH

In Halo 2 and Halo 3, the Plasma Rifle joins several other weapons which can be dual-wielded.

MANUFACTURER: Iruiru Armory
DESIGNATION: Type-25 Directed Energy Rifle
AMMUNITION: Superheated Plasma
ENERGY CAPACITY: 100 units
LENGTH: 24.5in (62.1cm)
FIRING MODE: Automatic

The Plasma Rifle is the standard rifle of all Covenant troop deployments due to its continued reliability in the field. It is customarily carried by Elite infantry as their primary sidearm.

Ammo counter

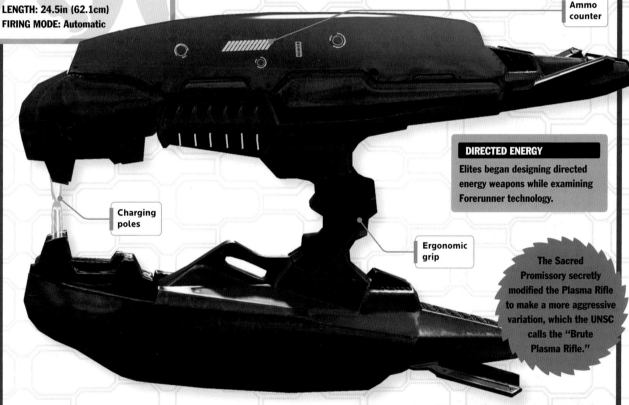

Charging poles

DIRECTED ENERGY

Elites began designing directed energy weapons while examining Forerunner technology.

Ergonomic grip

The Sacred Promissory secretly modified the Plasma Rifle to make a more aggressive variation, which the UNSC calls the "Brute Plasma Rifle."

RELIABLE SIDEARM

The Plasma Rifle is an effective short- to mid-range weapon with a reasonable rate of fire combined with a relatively shallow expenditure of energy. This makes the weapon both useful and less resource-intensive, which has made it a consistent part of the Covenant's infantry armament. While it was previously used by Elites with some exclusivity, it has also been carried into battle by a number of other species, namely Jackals and Brutes, the latter actually using a modified variant. While it is not the most powerful or most accurate weapon the Covenant have fielded, it has a simple, elegant design and a decent rate of fire.

PORTAL AT VOI
FORERUNNER EXCESSION SITE, EAST AFRICAN PROTECTORATE

The Portal is a Forerunner machine buried below the Earth, which generates a slipspace gateway. When activated by a keyship, the Portal opens, giving direct passage to the Ark installation.

STATISTICS

HALO 3 • HALO 3: ODST

In the Halo 3 mission "The Storm," the Prophet of Truth attempts to activate the Portal. Players must eliminate a Mantis anti-air gun that is blocking UNSC forces from their assault on Truth.

DESIGNATION: Forerunner Excession Site, East African Protectorate
SITES: Earth and other worlds
DIAMETER: 72.79 miles (117km)
FUNCTION: Conveyance across slipspace
COMPOSITION: Slipspace field generated by a massive gateway machine

HIDDEN FOR MILLENNIA

On October 20, 2552, the Covenant arrived on Earth and began looking for the Ark. Their means of accessing this mysterious site was by way of an ancient artifact buried below the planet's surface, which humanity would later refer to as the Portal. This machine could only be activated by a Forerunner keyship. After the Ark's destruction, the Portal closed and the site became a memorial to those who had perished.

Dreadnought

Portal

Pylon

POST-WAR ANALYSIS

The Portal, also known as the Excession, was researched extensively by humanity's top minds soon after it became dormant.

PROPHET OF MERCY

THE HIERARCH AND HIGH PROPHET OF MERCY

As a Philologist, Mercy served as an Ascetic priest, exploring the vast information pathways of the Forerunner Dreadnought.

The Prophet of Mercy was once the Covenant's leading Philologist. However, in 2525 he met two other Prophets, with whom he entered into a conspiracy that shook the Covenant to its core.

Hierarch crest

San'Shyuum waddle

RISE TO POWER

When the Covenant stumbled upon humanity, the horrific discovery of a flaw in their theology was made known to the Philologist: If the humans were, in fact, heirs to the Forerunner legacy, then the entire foundation of the Covenant was a lie. To maintain the fragile interspecies alliance, the Philologist joined in a conspiracy with two other Prophets and ascended to the station of Hierarch as the High Prophet of Mercy. Decades later, the truth about Halo, the Flood, and humanity's birthright was made known, bringing about a civil war and Mercy's demise.

STATISTICS

HALO 2

As the Master Chief, the player encounters Mercy firsthand at the start of the Halo 2 mission "High Charity."

FULL NAME: Hod Rumnt
SPECIES: San'Shyuum
RANK: Hierarch
HEIGHT: 7ft (215.9cm)
WEIGHT: 192.4lbs (87.3kg)
HOMEWORLD: High Charity
DATE OF BIRTH: August 22, 2332
DATE OF DEATH: November 3, 2552

Prehensile feet

THE GREAT SCHISM

Mercy's death came at the hands of the Flood as High Charity was engulfed by the parasite during the violent civil war known as the Great Schism.

PROPHET OF REGRET
THE HIERARCH AND HIGH PROPHET OF REGRET

The youngest of the three Hierarchs during the last Age of Reclamation, the Prophet of Regret was ambitious, brazen, and outspoken; all qualities that led to his end at the hands of the Master Chief.

Ceremonial crown

PERILOUS AMBITION

When he was Vice Minister of Tranquility, Lod Mron recognized a shared ambition in his superior, the Minister of Fortitude. Together, the two Prophets ascended to the rank of Hierarch by leveraging the discovery of humanity and using the Covenant war machine against this newfound species. As the High Prophet of Regret, Lod Mron worked with the Elites to obliterate every human world they found. Failing to seize control of the Portal to the Ark, Regret fled to Delta Halo, where he was swiftly tracked down and killed by the Master Chief.

STATISTICS

Contemporary raiment

Anti-gravity throne

HALO 2 • HALO WARS

In Halo 2's mission "Regret," the player is ordered to hunt and kill the Prophet.

FULL NAME: Lod Mron
SPECIES: San'Shyuum
RANK: Hierarch
HEIGHT: 7ft 2in (218.3cm)
WEIGHT: 204.1lbs (92.6kg)
HOMEWORLD: High Charity
DATE OF BIRTH: October 28, 2461
DATE OF DEATH: November 2, 2552

Regret served in many theaters of war, preferring to be in the midst of battle rather than in the safety of High Charity.

ESCAPING TO DELTA HALO

As the Master Chief approached Regret's ship above New Mombasa, the Prophet hastily fled, finding his way to the momentary safety of Delta Halo.

PROPHET OF TRUTH

THE HIERARCH AND HIGH PROPHET OF TRUTH

STATISTICS

HALO 2 • HALO 3 • HALO 3: ODST

Truth is finally captured and killed by the Arbiter and the Master Chief during the Halo 3 mission, "The Covenant."

FULL NAME: Ord Casto
SPECIES: San'Shyuum
RANK: Hierarch
HEIGHT: 7ft 3in (220.9cm)
WEIGHT: 201lbs (91.2kg)
HOMEWORLD: High Charity
DATE OF BIRTH: March 15, 2396
DATE OF DEATH: December 11, 2552

For decades, the Minister of Fortitude was an exceptional politician. Thanks to his cunning and machinations, he rose to the rank of High Prophet and eventually took full control of the Covenant.

Before joining the Ministry of Fortitude, Ord Casto began his political career in the Ministry of Concert, managing interspecies relations.

Personalized crown

POLITICAL MASTERMIND

When the Ministry of Tranquility stumbled upon the human species, the apparent heirs of the Forerunners, Truth took the opportunity and moved quickly to conceal the connection from the rest of the Covenant. Through political subterfuge, he rose to the position of Hierarch, leading the Covenant's genocidal campaign against the humans, until the discovery of the Halo rings revealed the truth about the Forerunners. In a last ditch effort to activate Halo from the Ark, Truth found his end at the hands of the Arbiter—the same one he had created only months earlier to protect his power.

THE COVENANT'S DOWNFALL

Truth's distrust of the Elites caused him to move against them at a critical hour. In turn, they aligned with the UNSC, tipping the scales in humanity's favor and ultimately destroying the Covenant.

PROWLER
TYPE-52 INFANTRY SUPPORT VEHICLE

The Prowler is a Brute-designed alternative to the Elite's Spectre. During the final months of the Covenant War, the Brutes used this vehicle extensively against the UNSC forces on Earth and across the Ark.

STATISTICS

HALO 3

Be wary of the Prowler in Halo 3's Campaign, as they typically appear carrying a handful of fully armed Brutes.

MANUFACTURER: Sacred Promissory
DESIGNATION: Type-52 Infantry Support Vehicle
CREW: 1 driver + 1 gunner + 2 passengers
LENGTH: 23.3ft (7.1m)
WIDTH: 13.8ft (4.2m)
PRIMARY ARMAMENT: Light Plasma Cannon

WELL-ARMORED

While The Prowler's dual suspension tracks constrict its movement, the heavy armor makes up for it.

Plasma Cannon

The Prowler was fielded prior to the Great Schism, but it was used most at the end of the war with the humans.

Suspension skids

DEVIOUS MACHINE

The T-52 ISV was crafted to support the Brute campaign against the humans, though much of its design was held over from their own technology on the planet of Doisac. Like other Brute weapons and vehicles, the Prowler is a crude modification of existing Covenant technology; in effect, scraps and debris bound together and engineered to meet the Brutes' own needs. Despite the light plasma cannon mounted atop its chassis, Brutes often prefer to use the vehicle's rigid and razor-sharp front end to violently cut down enemy infantry; a customary attribute of most Brute designs.

STATISTICS

HALO 2 • HALO: REACH

In Halo: Reach, players are tasked with the defense of the planet; a valiant though ultimately futile effort.

STAR, POSITION: Epsilon Eridani, II
SATELLITE(S): Csodasvarvas, Turul
GRAVITY: 1.08 G (approx)
ATMOSPHERE: 1 (N_2, O_2)
SURFACE TEMPERATURE: −15°F to 108°F (−26°C to 42°C)
DATE FOUNDED: 2362
MAJOR CITIES: Manassas, Quezon, Ezhtergom, New Alexandria
POPULATION: 703,341,500 (pre-war)
SPACE TETHERS: 9

In addition to being the largest nonautomated exporter of titanium, the planet of Reach was the literal center of the UNSC's naval might, home to a military complex unparalleled in both size and scope.

UNSC STRONGHOLD

Since its founding, Reach has been an important part of the UNSC. It is the largest naval yard within human-controlled space, a major exporter of titanium, and the training ground for some of the UNSC's most important soldiers. However, in 2552, all of that changed. The Covenant arrived, at first with advanced scouting parties, but later with a full-fledged invasion fleet on August 30, 2552. By then, it was only a matter of days before the entire planet would be completely destroyed.

GATEWAY TO EARTH

Due to its proximity to Sol, at roughly 10.5 light years, Reach is considered to be at the metaphorical doorstep to Earth.

Reach is only the fourth largest planet in the Epsilon Eridani system, though it is significantly larger than Earth.

Diameter: 9,490 miles (15,273km)

RECON ARMOR
MJOLNIR POWERED ASSAULT ARMOR/R—RECON

The Recon variant of armor was designed to increase a user's stealth abilities and it has performed exceptionally well for both Mark V and Mark VI platforms of MJOLNIR armor.

STATISTICS

HALO 3 • HALO 3: ODST • HALO: REACH

The Recon helmet is available from Halo: Reach's Armory by acquiring the rank of Colonel and purchasing it for 100,000 credits.

SERIES: Mark V/Mark VI
MANUFACTURER: Materials Group
TESTING SITE: B5D Ordnance Testing Facility

STEALTH ARMOR

Recon, like its parallel variant Scout, was developed at the B5D Ordnance Testing Facility in Swanbourne. The goal for Recon was to improve stealth infiltration with negligible loss of endurance, mobility, and other combat faculties. The Materials Group finalized this through the dramatic reduction of the armor's infrared signature and Cherenkov radiation emission.

B5D-R/ Optics Suite

T-31 Needle Rifle

Ceramic plating

Like other MJOLNIR variants, Recon can be integrated with modular attachments, offering uplink connectivity for on-the-fly intel.

WIDE APPEAL

Recon is not limited to MJOLNIR armor bases. Its architecture is also used by ONI and in body armor throughout the Navy and Marine Corps.

Mk. V— undersuit sheathing

STATISTICS

HALO WARS

Red Team was introduced in the mission "Arcadia City," and subsequently follows the player throughout the rest of the campaign.

PARTICIPANT: Jerome-092
HEIGHT: 7ft 2in (219.1cm)
WEIGHT: 290lbs (131.5kg)

PARTICIPANT: Alice-130
HEIGHT: 6ft 11in (211.6cm)
WEIGHT: 282lbs (127.9kg)

PARTICIPANT: Douglas-042
HEIGHT: 7ft 4in (223.8cm)
WEIGHT: 302lbs (136.9kg)

The status of this team is not known, but they were aboard the *Spirit of Fire*, which was officially declared "lost with all hands" on February 10, 2534.

Although the term "Red Team" could refer to other Spartan and non-Spartan squads, the one most well-known by that name is easily the Spartan team deployed to Arcadia in 2531.

FATEFUL MISSION

The SPARTAN-II assets formally categorized as "Red Team" fought in a number of campaigns during their first few years of service. In 2531, however, they found themselves on Arcadia, fighting alongside the crew of the UNSC *Spirit of Fire*. This conflict took them to a Forerunner shield world, where they battled the Covenant, the Flood, and were eventually forced to destroy the artificial planet to prevent the Covenant from using the ancient fleet it held. This act left the team stranded aboard the *Spirit of Fire*.

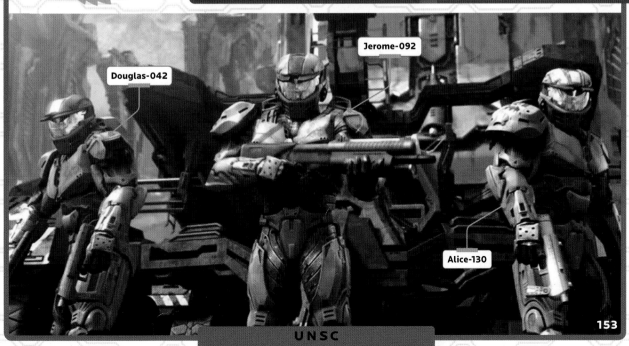

Douglas-042

Jerome-092

Alice-130

REVENANT
TYPE-48 LIGHT ASSAULT GUN CARRIAGE

The Revenant is a light-armored mobile artillery vehicle which simultaneously leverages the speed and maneuverability of a Ghost with a plasma mortar system similar to that of the Wraith.

Drivers should keep the Revenant in constant motion, as the operator and passenger seats are open to enemy fire.

MANUFACTURER: Merchants of Qikost
DESIGNATION: Type-48 Light Assault Gun Carriage
CREW: 1 operator + 1 passenger
LENGTH: 21.3ft (6.5m)
WIDTH: 13.2ft (4m)
PRIMARY ARMAMENT:
Medium Plasma Mortar

THE MOON OF QIKOST

One of the few vehicles manufactured by the Qikost-based Elite armory, the contemporary T-48 originates from an older, cruder Sangheili machine.

Plasma Mortar

The Revenant is known for its sleek contours, sturdy frame, and high speed—all borne out of the Covenant's innovative private sector.

Armored cowling

Anti-gravity system

INFANTRY SUPPORT

The functional gap between the Covenant's Ghost and Wraith has been filled many times over, mostly by infantry support vehicles like the Spectre and Prowler. However, the most effective vehicle in this area has historically been the Revenant, a midsize, light-armored assault vehicle capable of firing a Class-2 plasma mortar. Though its pilot cabin and passenger seat are exposed and unarmored, the vehicle's perfect marriage of speed and weaponry makes up for its relative lack of safety.

STATISTICS

HALO WARS

Several Rhinos are used to take down the Covenant's energy shield in the Halo Wars mission "Dome of Light."

MANUFACTURER: Chalybs Defense Solutions
DESIGNATION: M145D Mobile Artillery Assault Platform
CREW: 1 operator
LENGTH: 51.3ft (15.6m)
WIDTH: 29.4ft (9m)
PRIMARY ARMAMENT:
Prototype Zeus 320mm Cannon

From the cutting edge of development within ONI, the M145D MAAP, or "Rhino," was one of the first reverse-engineered Covenant technologies introduced by the UNSC into combat.

Rear lockdown system

Zeus 320mm Cannon

The Spirit of Fire borrowed a set of Rhinos from the Pillar of Autumn, as the two UNSC ships engaged the Covenant above the planet Arcadia.

Six tread tracks

LOCKDOWN MODE

The Rhino is notably wider than both the Scorpion and the Grizzly due to an unorthodox tread orientation that facilitates a lockdown mode before firing its 320mm weapon.

EXPERIMENTAL TECHNOLOGY

Amid the rubble and devastation that littered Harvest, ONI procured Covenant technology and immediately began reverse engineering it. Their results varied, but one project yielded the Rhino. The basis for this experimental technology, codenamed "Zeus," was a 320mm cannon affixed to the platform which could harness and direct plasma energy, similar to most Covenant weaponry. The Rhino saw impressive but limited use during the Covenant War, although the data gleaned from it was later used on other projects.

ROCKET LAUNCHER
M41 SSR MEDIUM ANTI-VEHICLE/ASSAULT WEAPON

In conventional ground warfare, no UNSC infantry weapon outweighs the raw stopping power and blast radius of the Rocket Launcher. Its brutal effectiveness has stood the test of time as a staple of the UNSC's armament.

STATISTICS

HALO: COMBAT EVOLVED • HALO 2 HALO 3 • HALO WARS • HALO 3: ODST HALO: REACH

The most effective way to eliminate infantry with the Rocket Launcher is to fire at the ground near an enemy's feet.

MANUFACTURER: Misriah Armory
SERIES: M41 SSR Medium Anti-Vehicle/Assault Weapon
AMMUNITION: M19 SSM 102mm High-Explosive Shaped-Charge
MAGAZINE CAPACITY: 2 rockets
LENGTH: 56.8in (144.3cm)
FIRING MODE: Semi-automatic

Twin barrels

Smart-linked sight

Shoulder mount

Two common field names for the Rocket Launcher are "Jackhammer" and "SPNKr."

Stabilizing grip

M19 SSM

Often confused with the M41, the M19 Surface-to-Surface Missile is an impressively powerful 102mm HESC ammunition.

POWERFUL INFANTRY WEAPON

The M41 Surface-to-Surface Rocket Launcher (Medium Anti-Vehicle/Assault Weapon) is the seasoned result of a long developmental history within the UNSC. As indicated by its design, the Rocket Launcher fires twin, self-propelled 102mm high-explosive shaped-charges. The blast force of these easily eliminates infantry threats, as well as most light vehicles. Many UNSC Rocket Launchers also have homing capabilities allowing the rockets to continue pursuit of a target even if it attempts an evasive maneuver.

ROCKET WARTHOG

M12 LIGHT ANTI-AIRCRAFT VEHICLE—ROCKET

While the Rocket Warthog looks like and handles similarly to the standard Warthog, its impressively destructive armament—the hulking twin M79 MLRS pods—dramatically set it apart from the traditional M12 FAV.

UNSC ARTILLERY

The Multiple Launch Rocket System, or MLRS, has always been a cornerstone of UNSC artillery, whether utilized for vehicles or emplacements.

FIERCE FIREPOWER

The purpose of a multiple launch rocket system is to overwhelm a target with force so destructive that nothing can survive. Combining raw firepower with the maneuverability and speed of a Warthog is a match made in heaven, hence the success of the Rocket Hog. It fires six 65mm Argent V Missiles at a target and can lock onto airborne craft if an encounter requires ground-to-air capabilities. Similar in many respects to the M9 Wolverine MAAT, the Rocket Hog shelves the secondary armament and armor for additional mobility and speed.

Other Rocket Warthog variants have been witnessed in combat, including the UNSC's M12A1 LAAV.

M79 MLRS

Hydraulic mounting system

Roll cage

ULED headlights

STATISTICS

HALO: REACH

The Rocket Hog premiered in Halo: Reach's mission "Tip of the Spear," where players eliminate Tyrants littering the canyon walls of Szurdok Ridge.

MANUFACTURER: AMG Transport Dynamics
DESIGNATION: M12 Light Anti-Aircraft Vehicle—Rocket
CREW: 1 driver + 1 gunner + 1 passenger
LENGTH: 19.7ft (6m)
WIDTH: 9.9ft (3m)
PRIMARY ARMAMENT: M79 Multiple Launch Rocket System

ROGUE ARMOR
MJOLNIR POWERED ASSAULT ARMOR/A—ROGUE

Created by the Vestol Corporation, the privatized Rogue variant of MJOLNIR armor eschews the traditional team-oriented technolgy of standard variants and caters to soldiers who primarily operate alone.

Mk. VI —VAS-R suite

MA5C Assault Rifle

CORPORATE BORN

Even before the Mark VI series went active in the fall of 2552, ONI had already reached out to private corporations with its schematics and specifications. The Vestol Corporation, known for its work in cybernetics and advanced theft-deterrent systems, yielded concrete results toward the end of the Covenant War. Based out of Bolvadin, Tribute, Vestol's "Rogue" variant was drawn from the "A" line of Mark VI specs. It was engineered to provide single operators with advanced network connectivity and sequentially delineated intel packets.

Rogue armor saw limited use at the close of the Covenant War, though reports indicate that it performed exceptionally.

STATISTICS

HALO 3

The Rogue armor is only available in Halo 3, after a player becomes a Spartan Officer.

SERIES: Mark VI
MANUFACTURER: Vestol Corporation
TESTING SITE: Vestol Simulation Lab

ROMEO
LANCE CORPORAL KOJO AGU

HALO 3: ODST

In the Halo 3: ODST mission "NMPD Headquarters," the player uses Romeo to defend his teammates' crash site.

FULL NAME: Kojo Agu
SERVICE NUMBER: 14606-85099-KA
BRANCH: UNSC Marine Corps
GROUP: Naval Special Weapons, Orbital Drop Shock Troopers
RANK: Lance Corporal
HEIGHT: 6ft 3in (190cm)
WEIGHT: 200lbs (91kg)
HOMEWORLD: Madrigal
DATE OF BIRTH: June 12, 2524

Kojo Agu, or "Romeo," was a dedicated ODST, a superb soldier, and above all, an excellent marksman. His skills proved useful throughout the war, particularly during the Covenant's siege of New Mombasa.

ODST-O/I combat helmet

SRS99D-S2 AM Sniper Rifle

EXPERIENCED MARKSMAN

Romeo joined the UNSC Marine Corps in 2541, where he served in numerous successive campaigns, eventually meeting Corporal Taylor "Dutch" Miles. After the conflict on Ariel, Romeo, and Dutch were transferred under the wing of Gunnery Sergeant Edward Buck, where they ran a top-secret operation right into the heart of the city of New Mombasa. During the battle that followed, Romeo was gravely injured by a Brute Chieftain near the NMPD headquarters building. Miraculously, he managed to stay alive as the remainder of his squad completed their objective.

To prevent excessive blood loss, Romeo's injury was filled with a biofoam polymer sealant.

ROOKIE
LANCE CORPORAL

Transferred from the 26th Marine Expeditionary Force, the ODST known as the Rookie joined a squad tasked with a highly classified operation in the besieged city of New Mombasa.

STATISTICS

HALO 3: ODST

Halo 3: ODST allows players to use several ODST characters, but the primary one is the lone Rookie.

FULL NAME: [CLASSIFIED]
SERVICE NUMBER: 11282-31220-JD
BRANCH: UNSC Navy
GROUP: Naval Special Weapons, Orbital Drop Shock Troopers
RANK: Lance Corporal
HEIGHT: 6ft 1in (186cm)
WEIGHT: 194lbs (88kg)
HOMEWORLD: Luna
DATE OF BIRTH: [CLASSIFIED]

NEW TO THE TEAM

Much of the Rookie's identity remains a mystery. What is known is that he served as part of a Rapid Offensive Picket in the 26th MEF. Shortly before the fall of 2552, he saw nearly all of his fellow troopers perish in New Jerusalem on Cygnus. Soon afterward, he was transferred to the ODST squad of veteran Eddie Buck for a classified operation. Unbeknownst to the Rookie at the time, their objective was the procurement of an ONI asset known as "Vergil." After being separated from his squad for several hours, the Rookie finally located both his men and the asset, narrowly escaping the Covenant's assault on the city.

Field pack

M7S SMG

Accessing various terminals in New Mombasa, the Rookie learned of a civilian named Sadie Endesha and of her search for her father.

CRITICAL ASSET

Vergil was a subroutine of the New Mombasa's Superintendent AI, which held crucial data about what the Covenant were after on Earth.

STATISTICS

HALO: REACH

During the Halo: Reach mission "Long Night of Solace," players use the Sabre to execute Operation: UPPER CUT.

DESIGNATION: YSS-1000 Prototype Anti-Ship Spaceplane
CREW: 1 pilot + 1 radar intercept officer
LENGTH: 80.7ft (24.6m)
WIDTH: 62.1ft (18.9m)
PRIMARY ARMAMENT: M1024 ASW/AC 30mm MLA
SECONDARY ARMAMENT: ST/Medusa Missile Delivery System

The Sabre is a powerful and versatile prototype spaceplane designed for surgical orbital combat. The craft is equipped with a heavy arsenal, but can still operate with impressive precision.

ST/Medusa Missile Pod

Cockpit

M1024 ASW/AC

The Sabre can be launched from a planet's surface without the use of conventional off-world transit.

CLASSIFIED SITES

The Sabre's confidential development program was conducted at a handful of research facilities, one of which was located on the beaches of Reach's Farkas Lake.

HIGHLY CLASSIFIED

The Sabre is built for the dual purposes of peak acceleration and maneuverability in orbital combat, and is able to accomplish feats that many ground-to-space-capable vessels cannot. Its armament is equally impressive, carrying twin M1024 ASW/AC 30mm MLAs and a pair of ST/Medusa Missile Pods. As such, this craft is intended specifically for lethal encounters, not simply to disrupt, disable, or maim targeted enemy ships. Despite remaining a heavily classified project, the existence of which was denied by three separate administrations, the Sabre's mission results speak for themselves and its success resonates through every conflict in which it is deployed.

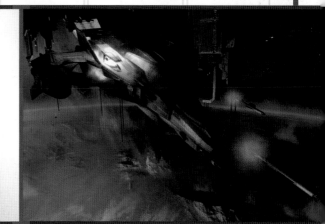

SAVANNAH
UNSC SAVANNAH FFG-371

The UNSC Savannah, a *Paris*-class frigate from Epsilon Eridani's local fleet, was called upon to make the ultimate sacrifice in a last ditch effort to end the *Long Night of Solace*'s reign of terror over Reach.

STATISTICS

HALO: REACH

Players fight alongside the UNSC *Savannah* and witness its brave sacrifice in the Halo: Reach mission "Long Night of Solace."

REGISTRY: FFG-371
CLASS: *Paris*-class Heavy Frigate
FLEET: Epsilon Eridani Fleet
COMMANDING OFFICER: Kristóf Jen
LENGTH: 1,755ft (535m)
BEAM: 652ft (199m)
PRIMARY ARMAMENT:
Magnetic Accelerator Cannon
SECONDARY ARMAMENT:
Missile Delivery System
TERTIARY ARMAMENT:
Point Defense System

MAC

The *Savannah* provided the much-needed point defense fire on the Covenant corvette *Ardent Prayer* and its Seraph escort.

Point Defense System

Titanium-A battle plating

EPSILON ERIDANI FLEET

The *Savannah*, like the many other ships within its fleet, was charged with the safety of the colonies in the Epsilon Eridani system. This included the planets Reach, Tribute, Circumstance, and a number of smaller human outposts.

SACRIFICE OF MANY

When Colonel Urban Holland approved Operation: UPPER CUT, he chose the UNSC *Savannah* to help in the strike on the Covenant ship the *Long Night of Solace* that was assaulting Reach. The *Savannah*'s slipspace drive was converted into an improvised ship-killing weapon. The frigate escorted the bomb to the *Ardent Prayer*, where Spartans seized control of the ship. Though the Covenant corvette was successfully used to carry the bomb to its target, the *Savannah* was sacrificed in the process.

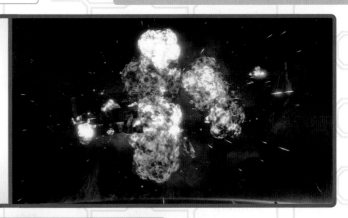

SCARAB

TYPE-47 ULTRA-HEAVY ASSAULT PLATFORM

STATISTICS

**HALO 2 • HALO 3 • HALO WARS
HALO 3: ODST • HALO: REACH**

In the Halo 3 multiplayer map "Assembly," players can see firsthand the creation of a Scarab within the Assembly Forges of High Charity.

MANUFACTURER: Assembly Forges
DESIGNATION: Type-47 Ultra-Heavy Assault Platform
CREW: 1 operator + 12 defenders
LENGTH: 159.5ft (48.6m)
WIDTH: 158.4ft (48.3m)
PRIMARY ARMAMENT:
Ultra-Heavy Focus Cannon
SECONDARY ARMAMENT:
Ultra-Heavy Plasma Cannon
TERTIARY ARMAMENT:
Type-52 Directed Energy
Support Weapon (3)

The Scarab is a heavily fortified and incredibly dexterous mobile platform that is capable of carrying Covenant infantry across varied terrain while armed with enough firepower to level an entire city.

Heavy Plasma Cannon

A LIVING MACHINE

The Scarab is actually composed of Lekgolo creatures, bound tightly into their colonial Mgalekgolo state. It is therefore more accurately defined as a single, ultra-heavy infantry unit rather than a "vehicle," despite the UNSC's formal classification.

Infantry platform

The Scarab's major weakness is a critical power juncture that exposes Lekgolo tissue, which is susceptible to weapon fire.

Interior bay

Heavy Focus Cannon

ATTACK PLATFORM

Originally designed for excavating Forerunner relics, Scarabs have since been fielded against humans. With the Lekgolo eels bound tightly together within the platform's armor, the Mgalekgolo collective can control the vehicle's movement and numerous weapons with little difficulty. Its primary weapon is a focus cannon, bolstered by a plasma cannon resting atop the carapace's stern. The Scarab can also carry up to 12 fully armed defenders and offers covering fire by way of three T-52 plasma cannons.

SCORPION
M808 MAIN BATTLE TANK

The Scorpion is one of the UNSC's most destructive and resilient armored vehicles. Dominant on the battlefield, it provides formidable firepower against most vehicles, earning it the respect of allies and enemies alike.

STATISTICS

HALO: COMBAT EVOLVED
HALO 2 • HALO 3 • HALO WARS
HALO 3: ODST • HALO: REACH

The Scorpion can carry four external passengers for additional protection.

MANUFACTURER: Chalybs Defense Solutions
DESIGNATION: M808 Main Battle Tank
CREW: 1 operator + 1 machine gunner
LENGTH: 33.6ft (10.2m)
WIDTH: 25.5ft (7.8m)
PRIMARY ARMAMENT: M512 90mm Smooth-Bore High-Velocity Cannon
SECONDARY ARMAMENT: M247 7.62mm Medium Machine Gun

Four-track configuration

M512 90mm SBHVC

M247 MMG

The Scorpion utilizes a four-track design for deft navigation. Each track is mounted on an independent suspension system.

TANK BEATS EVERYTHING

Forward Unto Dawn's Scorpion tanks powered through a massive Covenant blockade on the Forerunner Ark.

LONGSTANDING TANK

The M808 Scorpion is the most common main battle tank in the UNSC's arsenal, agilely balancing both mobility and firepower. Its primary M512 cannon can rotate 360 degrees and fire a 90mm SBHV tungsten shell, disintegrating most enemy targets in a single shot. To mop up infantry, the tank is also fitted with an M247 Medium Machine Gun, which can deliver 7.62mm armor-piercing rounds with both speed and thoroughness. Its prominence in the UNSC is a testament to its low production cost, its transportability, and its overall firepower.

SCOUT ARMOR
MJOLNIR POWERED ASSAULT ARMOR/S—SCOUT

A member of the heroic Noble Team, Jun-A266 used Scout armor when facing the Covenant on Reach.

The Scout armor variant was designed concurrently with Recon armor in an effort to improve stealth measures within the MJOLNIR platform, without limiting a user's mobility and endurance.

STATISTICS

HALO 3 • HALO: REACH

Players can acquire Halo: Reach's Scout helmet by achieving the rank of Captain and paying 40,000 credits.

SERIES: Mark V/Mark VI
MANUFACTURER: Materials Group
TESTING SITE: B5D Ordnance Testing Facility

ARMOR SPECIALIZATION

Spartans who use Scout tend to specialize in infiltration/reconnaissance and are often, but not exclusively, among the Spartan program's exceptional snipers.

Enhanced optics

MA37 Assault Rifle

COVERT OPERABILITY

Using nearly identical technologies, Scout and Recon were designed by the Materials Group based out of Swanbourne. Both variants attempted to reduce the infrared signature and Cherenkov radiation emitted by the user in order to increase the armor's stealth capabilities. Unlike Recon, however, the helmet architecture for Scout changed dramatically as the armor moved from the Mark V to Mark VI series. The Scout variant effectively serves Spartans across both the UNSC Army and Navy.

Titanium alloy shell

SCYTHE
M71 ANTI-AIRCRAFT GUN

Favored by UNSC bases across human-controlled space, the M71 Scythe was designed by Misriah Armory to be both powerful and reliable against a variety of airborne threats.

STATISTICS

HALO: REACH

Players are ordered to activate one of several M71 Scythe guns near the Airview Base during "ONI: Sword Base."

MANUFACTURER: Misriah Armory
SERIES: M71 Anti-Aircraft Gun
AMMUNITION: 20 x 102mm HEIAP
DRUM CAPACITY: 100,000 rounds
HEIGHT: 31ft (9.4m)
LENGTH: 27.9ft (8.5m)
FIRING MODE: Automatic

Barrels

Drum

The M71 Scythe was deployed at Sword and Castle bases on Reach, as well as at the Sabre launch facility on Farkas Lake.

Mount

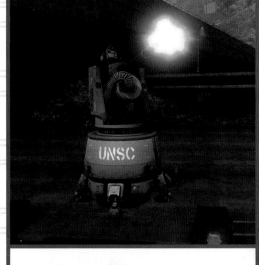

ANTI-AIR EFFECTIVENESS

The M71 Scythe Anti-Aircraft Gun, a drum-fed, pneumatically driven, air-cooled anti-aircraft weapon, was specifically designed to use the impressively potent 20mm High-Explosive Incendiary/Armor-Piercing (HEIAP) rounds. It can fire roughly 6,000 rounds per minute from six barrels, easily stripping away Covenant energy shields and armor, particularly on low-flying craft like Phantoms, Spirits, and Banshees. The M71 can be deployed on varied terrain and is usually tethered to an automated tracking system or defense-control AI, to provide a full range of fire on any airborne enemy craft.

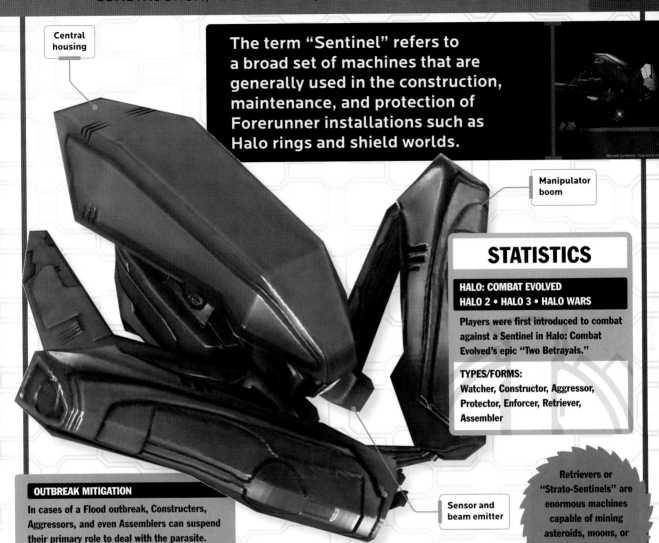

Central housing

Manipulator boom

Sensor and beam emitter

The term "Sentinel" refers to a broad set of machines that are generally used in the construction, maintenance, and protection of Forerunner installations such as Halo rings and shield worlds.

Microsoft Confidential - Trade secret or c

STATISTICS

HALO: COMBAT EVOLVED
HALO 2 • HALO 3 • HALO WARS

Players were first introduced to combat against a Sentinel in Halo: Combat Evolved's epic "Two Betrayals."

TYPES/FORMS:
Watcher, Constructor, Aggressor, Protector, Enforcer, Retriever, Assembler

OUTBREAK MITIGATION

In cases of a Flood outbreak, Constructers, Aggressors, and even Assemblers can suspend their primary role to deal with the parasite.

Retrievers or "Strato-Sentinels" are enormous machines capable of mining asteroids, moons, or other planetary bodies.

MANY ROLES

Designed in a variety of shapes and sizes to fit their many functions, Sentinels range from the diminutive Constructors, which effect repair and restoration, to the enormous Retrievers, which harvest resources from geological sites. Though a majority of a Sentinel's time is spent performing predetermined jobs, they can be retasked to deal with other situations, including a Flood outbreak. Aggressors are the most common Sentinel form, usually operating as a direct extension of the Monitor's will. No matter what their particular function may be, Sentinels play an important role in the Forerunners' plan.

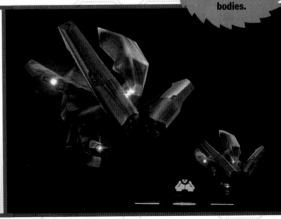

167

SENTINEL BEAM
CONTAINMENT/STERILIZATION INSTRUMENT

The Sentinel Beam is the primary weapon of Forerunner Sentinels. It shapes and directs beams of superheated particles, and is typically used to contain, sterilize, and eliminate Flood forms.

STATISTICS

HALO 2 • HALO 3

The Sentinel Beam was first seen in Halo: Combat Evolved, but only became playable in Halo 2.

SOURCE: Forerunner Sentinel
DESIGNATION: Containment/Sterilization Instrument
AMMUNITION: Superheated Particles
ENERGY CAPACITY: 100 units (dismounted)
LENGTH: 25.1in (63.7cm)
FIRING MODE: Automatic

Calibration dial

Battery housing

ENERGY CAPACITY

When attached to a Sentinel, a Sentinel Beam can fire indefinitely. Once separated, it normally has 100 units of energy.

Energy emitter

FORERUNNER WEAPON

Mounted on the undercarriage of a Sentinel, a Sentinel Beam is primarily used in the containment and sterilization of the Flood. Though little is known about its interior mechanics and design, its ammunition is based on negatively charged ions with low resource expenditure, shaped and directed into a beam of superheated particles. In cases where a Sentinel has been disabled, the weapon can be retrieved and fired by any user, although the machine will then have only a limited supply of ammunition.

Two of the most effective countermeasures against the Seraph are the OF92/EVA Booster Frame and the YSS-1000 Sabre.

The Type-31 XMF, classified as "Seraph," is the Covenant's primary multi-role, superiority fighter, performing impressively in both atmospheric and exoatmospheric conditions.

Propulsion system

STATISTICS

HALO 2 • HALO 3 • HALO: REACH

In the Halo 2 missions "The Arbiter" and "The Oracle," players battle on and around the armored hull of a Seraph.

MANUFACTURER: Assembly Forges
DESIGNATION: Type-31 Exoatmospheric Multi-Role Fighter
CREW: 1 pilot
LENGTH: 101.7ft (31m)
WIDTH: 49.7ft (15.1m)
PRIMARY ARMAMENT: Heavy Plasma Cannon (2)

ENERGY SHIELDING

The Seraph's energy shield will deflect and divert most missile and rocket delivery systems. However, it can be susceptible to well-placed gas-jacketed, armor-piercing rounds.

Cockpit

Plasma Cannon

COVENANT FIGHTER

The Seraph has operated at the front of most Covenant invasions and occupations, directly engaging enemies in a variety of conditions and providing fighter escort for Covenant fleets. Seraphs can coordinate strikes against planetside targets, organize reconnaissance and defense pickets, and engage in large-scale orbital combat against both enemy capital ships and A/X fighters. Armed with a pair of heavy plasma cannons and protected by an energy shield, the Seraph remains one of the Covenant's most effective and versatile crafts.

SERINA
SNA 1292-4

As the onboard AI construct of the UNSC *Spirit of Fire*, Serina played an important role in the ship's campaign on Harvest, Arcadia, and eventually the enigmatic Forerunner shield world.

STATISTICS

HALO WARS

In Halo Wars, Serina is used throughout the game's Campaign to direct and instruct the player.

SERIAL NUMBER: SNA 1292-4
ORIGIN: UNSC Navy
CLASS: Smart Artificial Intelligence
ROLE: Naval Support
ACTIVATION DATE: January 7, 2530

FRONTLINES OF THE WAR

Acquired by the UNSC *Spirit of Fire* in 2530, Serina was used in a variety of military operations before taking the ship to Harvest on a rescue mission for the UNSC *Prophecy*. Under the orders of Captain James Cutter, Serina deployed forces on Harvest's surface, and managed later campaigns on both Arcadia and a mysterious Forerunner shield world. It was here that Serina provided the first detailed analysis of the Flood. She also helped guide the *Spirit of Fire* around the shield world's imploding sun, allowing the vessel to escape the ensuing supernova.

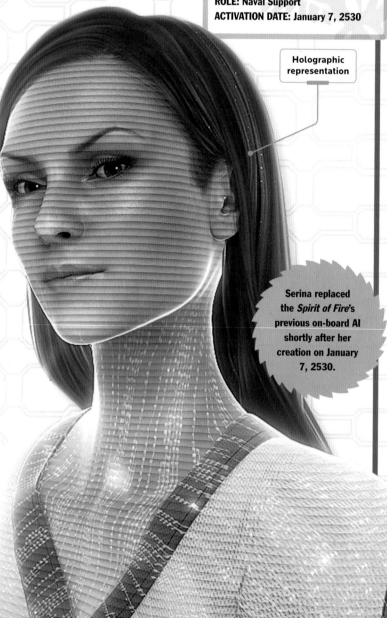

Holographic representation

Serina replaced the *Spirit of Fire*'s previous on-board AI shortly after her creation on January 7, 2530.

CONSTRUCT QUIRKS

Serina was often caustic and sardonic, particularly when it came to the civilian consultant Ellen Anders.

SHADE

TYPE-26 ANTI-INFANTRY STATIONARY GUN

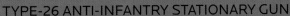

STATISTICS

HALO: COMBAT EVOLVED
HALO 2 • HALO 3 • HALO WARS
HALO 3: ODST • HALO: REACH

Halo: Reach showcases two different types of Shade: one plasma-based and the other fuel rod.

MANUFACTURER: Assembly Forges
DESIGNATION: Type-26 Anti-Infantry Stationary Gun
AMMUNITION: Superheated Plasma
ENERGY CAPACITY: Unlimited
HEIGHT: 10.1ft (3.1m)
LENGTH: 13ft (4m)
FIRING MODE: Automatic

This weapon has appeared in a variety of configurations, the most popular and effective of which is the Type-26 Anti-Infantry Stationary Gun. Shades are primarily used to suppress and eliminate enemy infantry.

The alternate T-29 Shade was used to great effect by the Fleet of Particular Justice during the conflict on Alpha Halo.

Flank protection

Firing channel

360-degree anti-gravity base

T-27 VARIANT

The T-27 Shade was present on the High Prophet of Regret's *Solemn Penance* and was employed both in New Mombasa and on Delta Halo.

STANDARD COVENANT TURRET

The term "Shade" refers to a platform of weapon emplacements with diverse configurations and functions, but they're all similar enough to be grouped together categorically. The 360-degree rotating Shade turret is an anti-personnel and ad hoc anti-matériel emplacement. The T-29 Shade sports a tripod leg system, has less armor, but provides greater mobility. The T-27 Shade consists of a mount, a seat, an energy shield, and is far more portable than other variants. The T-26 Shade has interchangeable components, allowing for the integration of fuel rod technology when necessary.

SHADOW
TYPE-29 TROOP/VEHICLE TRANSPORT

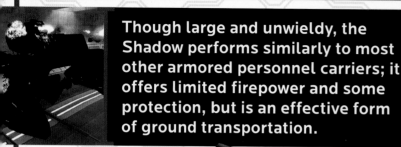

Though large and unwieldy, the Shadow performs similarly to most other armored personnel carriers; it offers limited firepower and some protection, but is an effective form of ground transportation.

The T-29 was deployed during the Covenant's occupation of New Mombasa in October 2552.

Rear ramp

Infantry compartment

ARMORED CONVOY

The mid-grade plasma armament does little to protect solitary Shadow transports, hence their need for accompanying vehicles and firepower.

Armored cabin

GROUNDSIDE TRANSPORTATION

The T-29 Shadow is used during protracted occupations, when planetside troop transportation cannot be performed with traditional dropships. It is extremely valuable in the narrow confines of dense urban areas and highway tunnel systems. Capable of carrying eight infantry or a light reconnaissance vehicle such as a Ghost, the Shadow performs its tasks nobly and with little difficulty. They rarely move alone and are usually seen with a light escort or in groups of five-to-ten transports.

The Fleet of Retribution that arrived at the Ark included one assault carrier and nine battlecruisers.

Seized by Rtas 'Vadum during the Great Schism, the *Shadow of Intent* led the Fleet of Retribution against the Prophet of Truth's Covenant forces above the Ark installation.

STATISTICS

HALO 3

Before the Halo 3 mission "The Ark," *Forward Unto Dawn* stows away within the enormous *Shadow of Intent*.

CLASS: CAS (Assault Carrier)
FLEET: Fleet of Retribution
SHIPMASTER: Rtas 'Vadum
LENGTH: 17,541ft (5,347m)
BEAM: 6,948ft (2,118m)
PRIMARY ARMAMENT:
Ventral Cleansing Beam
SECONDARY ARMAMENT:
Anterior Plasma Cannon
TERTIARY ARMAMENT:
Point Laser Defense

EXECUTING RETRIBUTION

Its history prior to the Great Schism remains a mystery, but what is known about the *Shadow of Intent* is that during the vicious internecine feud following the Prophets' betrayal of the Elites, Special Operations Commander Rtas 'Vadum engaged in combat with the Brutes and seized control of the *Shadow of Intent* and its fleet. 'Vadum used these vessels to pursue a Flood-infested cruiser back to Earth, where he followed the remaining Covenant forces to the Ark and brought ruin to the Prophet of Truth's fleets, aiding humanity in their darkest hour.

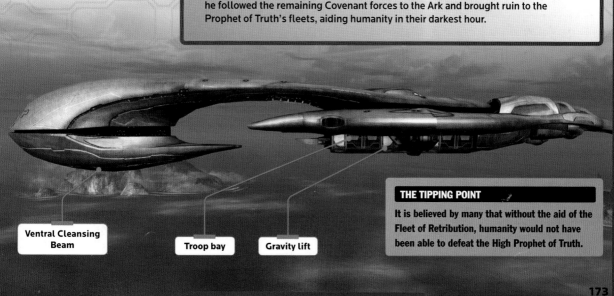

Ventral Cleansing Beam

Troop bay

Gravity lift

THE TIPPING POINT

It is believed by many that without the aid of the Fleet of Retribution, humanity would not have been able to defeat the High Prophet of Truth.

SHIELD WORLD
FORERUNNER SHIELD FACILITY 0459

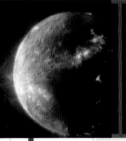

In February 2531, the UNSC *Spirit of Fire* found an artificial world created by the Forerunners. This huge installation, called Shield 0459, was a conservation sphere—a shield world built to protect select species from the Halo Array.

STATISTICS

HALO WARS

Though much of Halo Wars takes place on human colonies like Harvest and Arcadia, the latter portion of the game is played entirely on Shield 0459.

NAME: Shield 0459
STAR: Korinth Prior
GRAVITY: 0.998 G (approx)
ATMOSPHERE: 1.05 (N_2, O_2, Ar)
SURFACE TEMPERATURE: 50°F to 87°F (10°C to 31°C) (controlled)

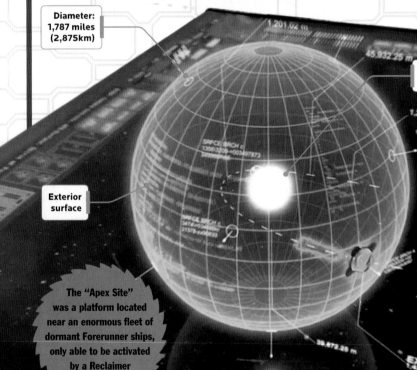

Diameter: 1,787 miles (2,875km)

Artificial sun

Exterior surface

The "Apex Site" was a platform located near an enormous fleet of dormant Forerunner ships, only able to be activated by a Reclaimer (human).

EXIT POINT

FORTIFIED PROTECTION

Shield 0459, like many other shield worlds, had an outer shell which remained sealed off from the fortified and protected interior—a vast, lush environment with an artificial star at its center.

ARTIFICIAL WORLD

The superstructure known as "Shield 0459," the fourth "planet" in the system Korinth Prior, became the site of a conflict between the UNSC and the Covenant. Within its expansive interior shell lay a hidden fleet of Forerunner warships that the Covenant fully intended to activate. Recognizing the threat this posed, the UNSC's *Spirit of Fire* sacrificed its slipspace drive in an effort to create a supernova using the shield world's artificial star. Shield 0459 was obliterated along with the Forerunner fleet and the local Covenant forces, though the *Spirit of Fire* narrowly escaped the devastation.

SHIPMASTER
SHIPMASTER RTAS 'VADUM

STATISTICS

HALO 2 • HALO 3

Players are able to fight alongside Rtas throughout Halo 2's campaign, as they play from the Arbiter's perspective.

FULL NAME: Rtas 'Vadum (previously 'Vadumee)
SPECIES: Sangheili
RANK: Shipmaster
MINISTRY: Ministry of Resolution (previously)
FLEET: Fleet of Retribution
HEIGHT: 7ft 11in (241.3cm)
WEIGHT: 323lbs (146.5kg)
HOMEWORLD: Sanghelios
DATE OF BIRTH: September 21, 2487

Originally a Special Operations (SpecOps) Commander in the Fleet of Particular Justice, Rtas 'Vadum became a shipmaster and played a pivotal role at the end of the Covenant War.

Combat-class helmet

GREAT WARRIOR

As SpecOps Commander, Rtas encountered the Flood aboard the Covenant ship *Infinite Succor*, where he lost his entire squad and his two left mandibles. This injury served as a constant reminder of the dangers the parasite held.

Assault-class pauldron

EXPERIENCED WARRIOR

Excelling in unconventional warfare, Rtas 'Vadumee became a SpecOps Commander for the Fleet of Particular Justice, serving under the leadership of Thel 'Vadamee. After the destruction of the first Halo ring, 'Vadumee was sent to Delta Halo to assist in its activation. During the course of this campaign, the Prophets and Brutes betrayed the Elites, splitting the Covenant in two. As this civil war raged on, Rtas seized command of the *Shadow of Intent* and the surviving Fleet of Retribution, and led it to the Forerunner Ark, while fighting alongside humanity. His efforts were crucial to the human victory against the Covenant.

Alloy-fused plating

SHORTSWORD
B-65 SUBORBITAL LONG-RANGE BOMBER

Although developed along the same lines as the GA-TL1 Longsword, the Shortsword bomber serves a much more specific purpose: ground support and air interdiction by way of precision bombing runs.

STATISTICS

HALO WARS

In Halo Wars, players can call in Shortsword bombing runs to soften enemy targets.

MANUFACTURER: Misriah Armory
DESIGNATION: B-65 Suborbital Long-Range Bomber
CREW: 1 pilot + 1 copilot + 1 systems technician
LENGTH: 89.6ft (27.3m)
WIDTH: 116ft (35.3m)
PRIMARY ARMAMENT: M955 ASW/AC 30mm MLA
SECONDARY ARMAMENT: Maastricht/Raleigh Ordnance Delivery-Application System

FIGHT FOR HARVEST

Several Shortsword bombers were fitted, repaired, and equipped on the UNSC *Spirit of Fire* during the Harvest campaign.

Winglet boom

M955 ASW/AC 30 MLA

M/RODAS

BOMBER OPTIMIZATION

Like the Longsword, the Shortsword has a moderately sized fuselage, broad swept-back wings for lift in-atmosphere, and a very heavy armament. Where this vessel differs from its larger brother is in the optimization of divergent ordnance delivery through M/RODAS (Maastricht/Raleigh Ordnance Delivery-Application System). Exclusive to this craft, the M/RODAS can drop a wide array of ordnance onto enemy targets, the most prominent of which are the Mark 208 550lb (249.7kg) bomb; the GBU-1105 (Guided Bomb Unit) 1,500lb (680.4kg) bomb, commonly known as the "cryo bomb;" and the XGBU-302 (Experimental Guided Bomb Unit) 4,000lbs (1,814kg) bomb, which can kill all electronic equipment within 2.1 miles (3.4km).

UNSC

The most common ammunition used with the Shotgun is the Soellkraft Hippo 8-gauge magnum shell.

The M45 Tactical Shotgun and, to a lesser degree, the M90 Close Assault Weapon System, offered the UNSC a powerful close-range arm during both the Insurrection and the conflict against the Covenant.

CLOSE-RANGE

The reliability and practicality of the shotgun remains unmatched in close-quarters combat. Championed by the UNSC during the rebellion and throughout the Covenant War, the M45 Tactical Shotgun and the M90 Close Assault Weapon System have both been critical fixtures in close-quarters combat scenarios, particularly when fighting in urban environments that have heavy enemy occupation. With six 8-gauge shells, the shotgun has incredible stopping power against both unshielded and shielded opponents.

Trigger

STATISTICS

HALO: COMBAT EVOLVED
HALO 2 • HALO 3 • HALO WARS
HALO 3: ODST • HALO: REACH

The shotgun's lethality at close quarters makes it much-sought-after on small, tightly designed multiplayer maps.

MANUFACTURER: Misriah Armory
DESIGNATION: M45 Tactical Shotgun
AMMUNITION: 8-Gauge Magnum
MAGAZINE CAPACITY: 6 shells
LENGTH: 46.4in (117.9cm)
FIRING MODE: Semi-automatic

M90 CLOSE ASSAULT WEAPON SYSTEM

Manufactured by Weapon System Technology, the M90 CAWS has really only one notable difference from the M45 and that is a higher magazine volume.

Front sight

Pistol grip

Forestock

SKIRMISHERS
KIG-YAR

Tougher and more agile than their same-species cousins, the Skirmishers offer another dimension to the Kig-Yar, which the Covenant are more than willing to employ against humanity.

STATISTICS

HALO: REACH

Skirmishers first appeared in Halo: Reach, though they had been part of the Covenant for some time.

SPECIES: Kig-Yar, *Perosus latrunculus*
HEIGHT: 6ft 2in to 6ft 9in (190cm to 206cm)
WEIGHT: 195lbs to 210lbs (88kg to 95kg)
HOMEWORLD: Eayn
TYPES/FORMS: Minor, Major, Murmillo, Ranger, Commando, Champion, Shipmaster, Shipmistress

PHYSICAL DIFFERENCES

Male Kig-Yar have varying degrees of plummage on their heads and necks, while females have a rigid set of scales instead.

ALTERNATE SPECIATION

Skirmishers originated on Eayn like their same-species cousins, the Jackals. They eventually came to colonize other locations within their system, an act which some have attributed as the reason for their distinctive physical differences. Others have suggested that these are a result of evolutionary distribution or genetic diversity. Skirmishers are used by the Covenant in a variety of fields of combat, though their troop allotment is not nearly as common as the Jackals'. Skirmishers played a large role in the invasion, occupation, and destruction of the planet Reach.

Heavy plumage

Avian scales

Not unlike Earth and Luna, the Kig-Yar's homeworld of Eayn and its gravity anchor, Chu'ot, are protected by an asteroid belt.

SNIPER RIFLE SYSTEM 99 ANTI-MATÉRIEL

STATISTICS

HALO: COMBAT EVOLVED
HALO 2 • HALO 3 • HALO WARS
HALO 3: ODST • HALO: REACH

Sniper Rifles can be used to destroy some of the most formidable vehicles in the Halo games.

MANUFACTURER: Misriah Armory
SERIES: Sniper Rifle System 99 Anti-Matériel
AMMUNITION: 14.5 x 114mm APFSDS
MAGAZINE CAPACITY: 4 rounds
LENGTH: 65.4in (166.1cm)
FIRING MODE: Semi-automatic

The Sniper Rifle entered service in the UNSC Army in 2460. Thanks to its incredible popularity, modular configuration, and manufacturer support, it was adopted by all branches by 2521.

LONG HISTORY

The origins of anti-matériel weapons like the SRS99 go as far back as World War I, with rifles specifically designed to penetrate tank armor.

Oracle scope

Grip

Barrel

Muzzle brake

All Spartans are trained in the use of SRS, though some specialize in this role like Linda-058 and Jun-A266.

Bipod

LONG-RANGE IMPLEMENT

Formally known as the Special Applications Rifle (SAP), the Sniper Rifle System 99 (SRS99) is primarily an anti-matériel weapon, though it has performed admirably against the Covenant's advanced shielding technology in an anti-personnel role. The rifle uses 14.5 x 114mm Armor-Piercing Fin-Stabilized Discarding Sabot (APFSDS) rounds that can easily penetrate and destroy enemy field equipment, vehicles, and even heavily armored Covenant soldiers, despite that not being its primary function.

SOLEMN PENANCE
FLEET OF SACRED CONSECRATION

The assault carrier *Solemn Penance* was at the head of the Covenant fleet that attacked Earth on October 20, 2552. It was led by none other than the High Prophet of Regret.

STATISTICS

HALO 2 • HALO 3: ODST

In Halo 2 and Halo 3: ODST, players witness the *Solemn Penance*'s jump into slipspace just above the city of New Mombasa.

CLASS: CAS (Assault Carrier)
FLEET: Fleet of Sacred Consecration
SHIPMASTER: Rhul 'Salmutee
LENGTH: 17,541ft (5,347m)
BEAM: 6,948ft (2,118m)
PRIMARY ARMAMENT:
Ventral Cleansing Beam
SECONDARY ARMAMENT:
Anterior Plasma Cannon
TERTIARY ARMAMENT:
   Point Laser Defense

The *Penance*'s Fleet of Sacred Consecration included 15 ships, two assault carriers, and 13 battlecruisers.

Propulsion system

CURRENT STATUS

The fate of the *Solemn Penance* is unknown, though some believe that it was subsumed back into High Charity's local fleets when the Covenant homeworld arrived at Delta Halo.

Hangar bay

Ventral Cleansing Beam

COVENANT FLAGSHIP

In search of a Forerunner Portal leading to the Ark, the Prophet of Regret led a Covenant fleet to Earth with its flagship *Solemn Penance* at the head. Once the fleet arrived, they quickly discovered that the planet was not only heavily populated by humans, but was the species' homeworld. Without hesitation, Regret ordered the *Penance* to the surface directly above the city of New Mombasa. However, as the Master Chief's presence drew nearer to his position, the Prophet feared for his life and escaped to Delta Halo, in the process creating a violent slipspace event that devastated the city.

SPADE

TURBOGEN INDEPENDENT WHEEL DRIVE SPADE

HALO: REACH

In Halo: Reach's "Winter Contingency," players can take the driver's seat of the Spade, with Jorge-052 in the flatbed, hefting his M247H onto the roll cage for additional firepower.

MANUFACTURER: TurboGen
DESIGNATION: TurboGen Independent Wheel Drive Spade
CREW: 1 driver + 1 passenger
LENGTH: 20.2ft (6.2m)
WIDTH: 10.3ft (3.1m)

Built for the brutal terrain of inhospitable colonial environments, the four-wheel drive Spade flatbed truck provides a versatile, economic, and rugged solution for outworld pioneers.

M96 methane engine

Rear bed

NOBLE TEAM

During their incursion in the farmlands of Visegrád, Noble Team commandeered Spades to track down a missing trooper squad.

Independent wheel drive

The name "Spade" likely originated from the domesticated Spadehorn, a bovid indigenous to Reach.

Towing cable

ALL-TERRAIN OPTION

The Independent Wheel Drive Spade is the most recent iteration in a long line of TurboGen all-terrain transports, a series of vehicles that have become an important part of life on the colonial frontier. The truck is primarily used by farmers and heavy-industry workers in environments which require rugged and versatile transportation. The Spade's M96 methane engine uses compound energy systems to power the vessel for prolonged use in physically demanding settings, and the truck also offers a large flatbed for transporting equipment and supplies. The vehicle comes in a variety of colors and configurations.

SPARROWHAWK
AV-22 SPARROWHAWK

The AV-22 Sparrowhawk is an aerodyne vehicle, first introduced into the UNSC in 2531, a number of years after its smaller precursor, the AV-14 Hornet. Its armament and mobility make it a significant threat.

The AV-22 Sparrowhawk is sometimes referred to in shorthand as the "Hawk."

ALTERNATE NOMENCLATURE

The Sparrowhawk is designated as an "Attack VTOL," though with its medium machine gun and nonlinear cannon, some branches of the UNSC have alternately classified it as a gunship.

M6 Nonlinear Cannon

Cockpit

GAU-23/AW/ Autocannons

STATISTICS

HALO WARS

The Sparrowhawk is seen throughout Halo Wars and exists within the hero unit loadout of Ellen Anders as an upgrade to the Hornet.

DESIGNATION: AV-22 Sparrowhawk
CREW: 1 pilot + 1 gunner
LENGTH: 54ft (16.5m)
WIDTH: 31.4ft (9.6m)
PRIMARY ARMAMENT: GUA-23/AW/Linkless Feed Autocannon (2)
SECONDARY ARMAMENT: W/AV M6 Grindell/Galilean Nonlinear Cannon

AERODYNE ARSENAL

Deployed toward the end of the conflict on Harvest, the Sparrowhawk met with great success in the war against the Covenant. The aerodyne's arsenal includes twin GAU-23 autocannons which fire 30mm rounds, and a powerful, chin-mounted M6 G/GNC that is an upgraded variant of the Spartan Laser. Despite its success, the Sparrowhawk's heavy cost for repair and replacement meant limited production after 2550.

SPARTAN LASER
WEAPON/ANTI-VEHICLE M6 GRINDELL/GALILEAN NONLINEAR RIFLE

STATISTICS

HALO 3 • HALO WARS
HALO 3: ODST • HALO: REACH

When firing the Spartan Laser, a player must sight and follow the target by holding down the trigger, allowing the weapon to charge before firing.

MANUFACTURER: Misriah Armory
SERIES: Weapon/Anti-Vehicle M6 Grindell/Galilean Nonlinear Rifle
AMMUNITION: Directed Energy
ENERGY CAPACITY: 4 to 5 shots
LENGTH: 47.7in (121.1cm)
FIRING MODE: Semi-automatic

Developed as part of the GUNGNIR project and alongside the MJOLNIR and SPARTAN-II programs, the Spartan Laser is a powerful and versatile shoulder-mounted directed-energy heavy weapon.

The Spartan Laser has gone through several iterations, but its changes have been mostly cosmetic.

SPARTAN ORIGINS

The name "Spartan Laser" originates from the project's links to SPARTAN-II. Though designed for Spartans, the weapon can be used by standard infantry as well.

Wyrd III smart-linked optics

Laser diode

Shoulder mount

Forward grip

NONLINEAR WEAPONRY

The central purpose of the GUNGNIR program was the creation of a heavy, non-ballistic weapon that could be fielded by infantry in an anti-matériel capacity. Working with both the SPARTAN-II and MJOLNIR research teams, GUNGNIR created a pinpoint-accurate nonlinear laser rifle that could fire its directed beam at 983,571,056 feet per second (299,792,458 meters per second). This firing velocity, when combined with the smart-linked Wyrd III optics suite for precision targeting, makes the M6 Spartan Laser a weapon of unparalleled value.

SPECTRE
TYPE-46 INFANTRY SUPPORT VEHICLE

The T-46 Spectre is one of a number of vehicles the Covenant employ to support infantry in combat. It was used with some success in the conflicts that took place on Earth and Delta Halo in 2552.

REPLACED

In the final weeks of the Covenant War, the Brute-designed T-52 ISV, also known as the Prowler, replaced the Spectre entirely.

Light Plasma Cannon

The Spectre's lateral mobility, its protected operator seat, and its rear-mounted turret are its key advantages against the Brute Prowler.

Gunner's mount

Operator seat

Anti-gravity propulsion

LIGHT TRANSPORTATION

First observed in 2546 during the Battle of Sargasso, the Spectre consists of a light-armored operator station flanked by two anti-gravity generators, each of which can support an additional passenger and whatever firepower they bring along with them. This aspect of transportability, combined with the Spectre's rear-mounted light plasma cannon, its speed, and its ability to deftly navigate the battlefield, provide the Covenant with a quick, versatile infantry support option on the frontlines of combat.

SPIKE GRENADE
TYPE-2 ANTIPERSONNEL FRAGMENTATION GRENADE

While the Spike Grenade may be considered a relic by Elites, Brutes appreciate its ability to instill terror in an enemy.

The Spike Grenade is a Claymore-like explosive that is designed to be thrown and impaled into hard surfaces or infantry personnel before detonating with expectedly horrific results.

BARBAROUS MUNITIONS

The Spike Grenade's basic function is very similar to that of the 20th-century Claymore mine: a fixed explosive which, upon detonation, launches projectiles at enemy personnel. Unlike the mine however, the Spike Grenade has an elongated baton-like shape, allowing it to tumble through the air when thrown. Once the grenade's momentum brings it in contact with a surface, its protrusions embed in the target, priming the grenade and detonating it on a fixed fuse. The Spike Grenade's explosion is directed conically from the point of impact, its contents effectively shredding anything in its path.

Grip

Shrapnel filler

Tactile protrusions

STATISTICS

HALO 3 • HALO 3: ODST

The Spike Grenade appears only in Halo 3 and Halo 3: ODST.

MANUFACTURER: Sacred Promissory
DESIGNATION: Type-2 Antipersonnel Fragmentation Grenade
FILLER: Shrapnel and a pyrophoric sulfur-nitrate/potassium compound of alien origin (shaped charge)
LENGTH: 36.7in (93.3cm)
KILLING RADIUS: 9.8ft (3m)
CASUALTY RADIUS: 36ft (11m)

SHAPED CHARGE

While the blast from a Spike Grenade extrudes away from its point of contact due to it being a shaped charge, the explosive force usually kills any unarmored individual within 10 feet (3 meters).

SPIKE RIFLE
TYPE-25 CARBINE

Although the Spike Rifle or "Spiker" fires its alien alloy spikes at a low muzzle velocity, its accuracy —and more importantly its overall durability—has stood the test of time on the battlefield.

STATISTICS

**HALO 3 • HALO 3: ODST
HALO: REACH**

Unlike most weapons in Halo, the Spike Rifle's ammunition can be ricocheted off many hard, flat surfaces when fired at the appropriate angle.

MANUFACTURER: Sacred Promissory
DESIGNATION: Type-25 Carbine
AMMUNITION: Superheated
Alien-alloy Spikes
MAGAZINE CAPACITY: 40 rounds
LENGTH: 32.2in (81.7cm)
FIRING MODE:
Automatic

The weapon's spike ammunition remains mysterious. Its alien origin on Doisac obfuscates any efforts to determine its composition.

Barrel

Bayonet

Grip

BRUTE WEAPON
The Spiker was seen early in the Covenant War, then was largely absent until late 2552, when Brutes returned to the Covenant's frontlines.

MERCILESS WEAPONRY

The Spike Rifle was originally designed by the Brutes on their homeworld of Doisac during their violent history, though its primitive form and function have been augmented to some degree by Covenant technology. Nevertheless, the weapon's core strength remains its incredibly lethal, vicious ammunition type and twin bayonets used to horrifically maim its victim. The purpose of this weapon is not only to harm and kill, but to invoke fear and terror in any who might meet it in battle.

STATISTICS

HALO: COMBAT EVOLVED
HALO WARS • HALO: REACH

In Halo: Reach, the Spirit dropship is indestructible, making it a slightly larger threat than the Phantom.

MANUFACTURER: Assembly Forges
DESIGNATION: Type-25 Troop Carrier
CREW: 1 pilot + 30 passengers
LENGTH: 108.4ft (33m)
WIDTH: 59.5ft (18.1m)
PRIMARY ARMAMENT:
Heavy Plasma Cannon

One of the most common Covenant dropships is the Spirit: A large, dual-bay deployment vessel which has a ventrally mounted force-field anchor used for transporting large machines and vehicles.

Tow field

PLASMA CANNON

The Spirit's ball-mounted plasma cannon provides a full range of coverage while deploying troops, though it is mostly used for suppressing groundside resistance.

Cockpit

Troop bay

Plasma Cannon

As with many Covenant ships and vehicles, the operator's cabin is placed away from the prow of the craft in order to protect the pilot.

CLASSIC DROPSHIP

With its unique profile and hull architecture, the Spirit is an instantly recognizable part of the Covenant's force. The main cabin sits toward the rear of the vessel with a ball-mounted heavy plasma cannon affixed to its undercarriage. The Spirit's most interesting attribute, however, is its twin troop bays which extend forward and out from the craft's main chassis, and are capable of carrying up to 30 soldiers. Explicit in their design, these secured harness stations allow the Spirit to perform extraordinarily aggressive maneuvers without endangering passengers.

SPIRIT OF FIRE
UNSC SPIRIT OF FIRE CFV-88

Built in 2473, the UNSC *Spirit of Fire* carried humanity to new worlds. However, during the Insurrection, the ship was refitted to be combat-effective against the rebel forces, inadvertently preparing it for the Covenant War.

HALO WARS

The *Spirit of Fire* gives players support throughout the entirety of Halo Wars.

REGISTRY: CFV-88
CLASS: *Phoenix*-class Support Vessel
FLEET: Third Fleet
COMMANDING OFFICER: James Cutter
LENGTH: 8,202ft (2,500m)
BEAM: 2,625ft (800m)
PRIMARY ARMAMENT:
Magnetic Accelerator Cannon
SECONDARY ARMAMENT:
Missile Delivery System
TERTIARY ARMAMENT:
Point Defense System

The *Spirit of Fire* belonged to Battlegroup D within Vice Admiral Cole's Third Fleet.

MAC

Bridge

Slipspace drive

LOST WITH ALL HANDS

Under the command of Captain James Cutter, the *Spirit of Fire* headed into the Covenant War in Vice Admiral Preston Cole's fleet during the campaign to recover Harvest from the Covenant. In 2531, the ship found and pursued Covenant forces who were searching for something buried below the northern regions of the planet. This pursuit led them to Arcadia and later to a Forerunner shield world, where they stopped the Covenant's plans to use an ancient fleet against humanity. This victory left the ship stranded without a slipspace drive to bring it home, and it was eventually declared "lost with all hands" by the UNSC.

SUBMACHINE GUN
M7/CASELESS SUBMACHINE GUN

The M7 SMG has a maximum effective range of about 164ft (50m).

A staple of the UNSC for decades, the M7 SMG played a vital role during the Insurrection and later in the Covenant War, notably in the fight for New Mombasa and during the conflict on Delta Halo.

Muzzle

Collapsible stock

SLS/V 5B

Silencer

STATISTICS

HALO 2 • HALO 3 • HALO 3: ODST

The SMG returned in Halo 3: ODST, offering players a silencer and a smart-linked scope for the first time on this weapon.

MANUFACTURER: Misriah Armory
DESIGNATION: M7/Caseless Submachine Gun
AMMUNITION: 5 x 23mm Caseless
MAGAZINE CAPACITY: 60 rounds (varies by model)
LENGTH: Retracted stock: 18.7in (47.4cm);
Extended stock: 24.7in (62.7cm)
FIRING MODE: Automatic

M7S VARIANT

Some M7S models are equipped with a smart-linked scope (SLS/V 5B), a component usually reserved for single-fire or burst-fire weaponry.

CLOSE-QUARTERS SOLUTION

The gas-operated, magazine-fed M7/Caseless SMG is one of the most popular weapons used by the UNSC in current combat operations. Efficient in close-quarters, it offers a clean, short-range solution against enemy infantry, particularly unshielded ones. The recoil is negligible in most cases, though it must be controlled by the operator. A variant of the standard SMG, the M7S, utilized by commando teams, incorporates sound suppression (SS/M 49).

SUBSTANCE
COELEST IV

All Halo ringworlds orbit a planetary giant that provides a gravitational anchor for the superstructure. Delta Halo's gravity anchor is the impressive ice giant called Substance.

Methane gas

HALO 2

Players can see the beautiful and majestic face of Substance during Halo 2's cinematics, as both High Charity and Delta Halo orbit in close proximity to it for most of the game.

STAR, POSITION: Coelest, IV
SATELLITE(S): 8
RELEVANCE:
Gravity Anchor for Installation 05
GAS COMPOSITION: H_2, He, CH_4
LIQUID COMPOSITION: NH_3, H_2O

Diameter:
51,418 miles
(82,749km)

RARELY SEEN

Substance is an enormous planet, but due to the tempestuous weather conditions of Delta Halo caused by a Flood outbreak centuries ago, it is infrequently visible from the ring's surface.

Exactly why the Forerunners chose gas and ice giants like Substance, for the purpose of the Halo Array, remains a mystery.

DELTA HALO SITE

Over six times the size of Earth, Substance is an ice giant located in the outer bands of the Coelest system. It is unknown why the Forerunners chose it, other than because of the system's relative locational value in its alignment with the six other Halo rings and its suitable orbital conditions. Delta Halo is one of eight satellites that orbit the largely gaseous planet. In fact, only one of Substance's satellites is a natural moon; the others are dormant Forerunner research facilities on predetermined orbital paths.

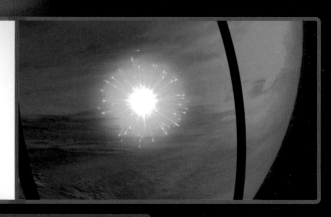

SUPERINTENDENT

NM/EAP/98458930-1244

STATISTICS

HALO 3: ODST

Throughout Halo 3: ODST, the Superintendent provides the player with direction, instruction, and insight into the events which befell New Mombasa hours earlier.

SERIAL NUMBER:
NM/EAP/98458930-1244
ORIGIN: City of New Mombasa
CLASS: Dumb Artificial Intelligence
ROLE: Urban Infrastructure
ACTIVATION DATE:
December 19, 2512

All six of Earth's space tether cities have a Superintendent AI to monitor them. The New Mombasa Superintendent is notable because it stumbled upon the Forerunner structure buried under the city.

Sad expression

TWO-DIMENSIONAL CONSTRUCT

Unlike many AI constructs, the Superintendent did not have a three-dimensional holographic representation: It manifested itself in a variety of simple but emotive two-dimensional expressions.

The Superintendent guided the Rookie to its data core, allowing the ODST to complete his mission objective and recover the intel the AI held.

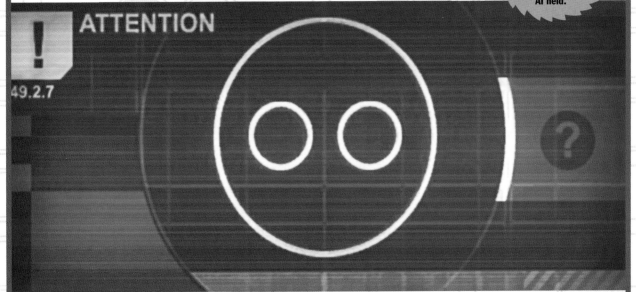

! ATTENTION

49.2.7

CITY MONITOR

The Superintendent of New Mombasa was a second-generation "dumb" AI who, just like other urban infrastructure constructs, managed a vast array of municipal functions. New Mombasa's AI, however, carried a special subroutine named "Vergil," designed by its architect, Doctor Endesha. Vergil was built to care for Endesha's daughter, Sadie, though during the Covenant's occupation it was used for much more. The Covenant targeted the Superintendent's data core after a recent seismic scan revealed a buried alien artifact. A Covenant Engineer extracted this data from Vergil, but later delivered it back to humanity.

CRITICAL ERROR (MEMCORE 530.21 OFFLINE)
EMERGENCY SHUTDOWN INITIATED

DATA TRANSFER COMPLETE

-----ERR-]]---
-----ERR-]]---

SWORD BASE
OFFICE OF NAVAL INTELLIGENCE, SWORD BASE

Sword Base, a highly classified ONI site hidden among the icy mountains of Babd Catha on Reach, provided direct access to a secret underground research facility tasked with the investigation of a buried Forerunner artifact.

Across Eposz there were several other research sites that investigated the artifact's debris field, including Castle Base.

KEY MILITARY BASE

The ONI site known as Sword Base contained an air field, an old communications relay called Farragut Station, and a heavily fortified main tower that included an atrium and a number of laboratories. Sword Base's true value, however, lay buried deep underground. Connected to the base by a tram system was an enormous chasm holding an ancient Forerunner artifact. For years, ONI had conducted extensive research on it, attempting to learn its secrets. On August 29, 2552, Sword Base was destroyed in order to keep these same secrets safe from the encroaching Covenant.

STATISTICS

HALO: REACH

Sword Base appears throughout Halo: Reach's Campaign, multiplayer, and Firefight modes.

DESIGNATION: Office of Naval Intelligence, Sword Base
LOCATION: Babd Catha Ice Shelf, Eposz, Reach
OFFICIAL PURPOSE: Air field, defensive stronghold, research facility
CONFIDENTIAL PURPOSE: Data aggregator for proximal alien artifact

ANCIENT ARTIFACTS

ONI was fully aware that the artifact near Sword Base was not the only vestige of the Forerunner civilization on Reach. Sites at Visegrád, in the Highlands, and across the entire Viery territory had also been discovered.

STATISTICS

HALO: REACH

The Target Locator is best used in a predictive fashion, leading moving targets since a hailed strike may take a moment to manifest.

MANUFACTURER: Misriah Armory
DESIGNATION: H-165 Forward Observer Module
LENGTH: 12.6in (32cm)

The Target Locator is used to sight and designate enemy targets from range, calling down fire support from an array of air or orbital vessels. These can be heavy or light, depending on the target in question.

FIRE SUPPORT

The purpose of the H-165 FOM is the coordinated neutralization of a given target, something usually accomplished by a surgical missile strike, a bombing run, or a hypersonic MAC round. The Target Locator is typically used by a Joint Fires Observer (JFO), though any UNSC soldier with appropriate clearance and training can use it to call in artillery support. When operating the module, an observer sights the target at a minimum safe distance, locking in the location with the fire support group. The ordnance is then deployed at the specified location, effectively neutralizing the target.

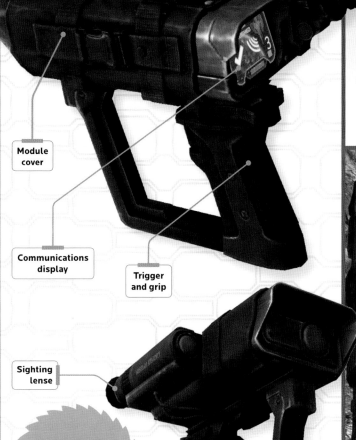

Module cover

Communications display

Trigger and grip

Sighting lense

The H-165 Forward Observer Module has two primary field uses: close air support and air interdiction.

MINIMUM SAFE DISTANCE

"Minimum safe distance" may be defined differently depending on the type of fire support used; JFO operatives are extensively trained to make such judgements.

TARTARUS
CHIEFTAIN OF THE BRUTES

In his youth, the Brute Tartarus witnessed firsthand the unfair treatment of his species by the Elites. Fueled by dedication and zeal, he engineered a meteoric rise within the Covenant.

ORIGIN OF HATE

As a whelp, Tartarus saw the integration of his civilization into the Covenant and later, their denigration under the Elites, which resulted in an unrelenting hate between the two species.

Familial pauldron

Warrior bandolier

RISE OF THE BRUTES

When Tartarus' uncle, the chieftain known as Maccabeus, first encountered the humans on Harvest, he underestimated the threat of the new species, which cost him the lives of several in his pack. For this failure, Tartarus ended his uncle's life, and took on the mantle of chieftain, earning him a place of prominence among the Brutes. For decades, Tartarus continued to loyally and violently serve as chieftain. He eventually came to the attention of the High Prophet of Truth, who used him to lead a civil war against the Elites in an effort to activate Delta Halo. This was not to be, however, as the Arbiter, who Tartarus had betrayed only hours earlier, returned to slay the chieftain and prevent Halo's activation.

Before its destruction, Alpha Halo was at the Lagrange point between Threshold and its impressive lunar satellite, Basis.

At the heart of the Soell system lies Threshold, an enormous gas giant which was once orbited by Alpha Halo, but is now only company to the debris field left in the ring's destruction.

Hydrogen/helium composition

ALPHA HALO SITE

Threshold is the seventh and largest planet of the Soell system. This enormous gas giant is similar in composition to Jupiter and in the past has had as many as 12 orbiting satellites, a number of which were Forerunner installations. Despite the generally inhospitable conditions of Threshold proper, both Installation 04 and the local gas mining facilities once offered the Forerunners safe havens in which they could research the Flood.

Diameter:
133,348 miles
(214,604 km)

STATISTICS

HALO: COMBAT EVOLVED • HALO: REACH

In Halo: Combat Evolved, Threshold can be seen looming in the skies above the first Halo ring.

STAR, POSITION: Soell, VII
SATELLITE(S): 12
RELEVANCE: Gravity Anchor for Installation 04
GAS COMPOSITION: H_2, He, CH_4
LIQUID COMPOSITION: NH_3, H_2O

MANY MOONS

Although Threshold's other moons were significantly smaller than Basis, the Forerunners still managed to utilize them for various purposes.

TROOP TRANSPORT
M831 TROOP TRANSPORT

One of the many Warthog variants, the M831 Troop Transport is unique in that it has no armament and is strictly used for transportation. Rather than a manned weapon in the rear bed, it has an expanded seating compartment.

STATISTICS

HALO 3 • HALO: REACH

Near the start of Halo: Reach's "ONI: Sword Base," players who move quickly can snag the escaping Troop Transport before the Covenant destroy it.

MANUFACTURER: AMG Transport Dynamics
DESIGNATION: M831 Troop Transport
CREW: 1 driver + 4 to 10 passengers
LENGTH: 19.7ft (6m)
WIDTH: 9.9ft (3m)

OFFENSIVE CAPABILITY

Though it is rare, the Troop Transport can serve as a lethal offensive vehicle with properly armed crew and passengers covering nearly all angles at any given time.

SLED spot light

Driver's seat

Rear bed seating

All-wheel drive

The Troop Transport supports various rear-bed configurations. The most common, the central aisle, allows passengers line of sight in almost all directions.

TROOP TRANSPORTATION

The Troop Transport Warthog has always been an important part of the UNSC's field equipment, but it is rarely seen in direct combat due to its obvious lack of weaponry. Optimal crew capacity is four passengers, but some M831 Warthogs can seat up to ten. Though armed soldiers can fight from the vehicle, this variant of Warthog is typically used to quickly ferry troops from one groundside location to another.

TRUTH AND RECONCILIATION

Prow

The battlecruiser known as the *Truth and Reconciliation* was part of the Covenant fleet which pursued the UNSC *Pillar of Autumn* from Reach and discovered Alpha Halo.

Energy shielded outer hull

First Lieutenant Melissa McKay destroyed the *Truth* to stop Major Antonio Silva from bringing a dangerous Flood specimen back to Earth.

Gravity lift

COVENANT BATTLECRUISER

Arriving in the Soell system in pursuit of the UNSC *Pillar of Autumn*, the *Truth and Reconciliation* was shot and severely damaged in the fracas. The ship was forced to seek safety on the surface of Halo, where it was used as a command-and-control station for the local Covenant forces. When the *Autumn*'s commanding officer, Captain Jacob Keyes, was captured by the Covenant, they transported him to the *Truth* for interrogation. However, their success was short-lived: The Master Chief and Cortana soon infiltrated the battlecruiser and retrieved the captain.

STATISTICS

HALO: COMBAT EVOLVED

In the Halo: Combat Evolved mission "Truth and Reconciliation," players storm through the corridors of the battlecruiser to rescue Captain Keyes.

CLASS: CCS (Battlecruiser)
FLEET: Fleet of Particular Justice
SHIPMASTER: Lat 'Ravamee
LENGTH: 5,847ft (1,782m)
BEAM: 2,827ft (862m)
PRIMARY ARMAMENT:
Ventral Cleansing Beam
SECONDARY ARMAMENT:
Anterior Plasma Cannon
TERTIARY ARMAMENT:
Point Laser Defense

TYRANT
TYPE-38 ANTI-AIRCRAFT CANNON

The Tyrant is an ultra-heavy anti-aircraft weapon, frequently used to fortify a location. Although difficult to transport and deploy, its impressive firepower easily makes up for such disadvantages.

TURNING THE TABLES

Once a Tyrant has been neutralized and its Covenant occupants eliminated, UNSC forces can use its base as a makeshift fortification against the very enemies who erected it.

FORMIDABLE EMPLACEMENT

The Type-38 Tyrant is yet another component of the Covenant's occupation stratagem: It is a large artillery emplacement intended to fortify local infantry, provide a guarded elevation for marksmen, and, most importantly, offer an aggressive anti-air solution in the form of an ultra-heavy plasma cannon. Typically, this weapon fires three rapid shots, providing a higher overall accuracy rate per volley than the T-27 Mantis emplacement.

STATISTICS

HALO: REACH

In the Halo: Reach missions "Tip of the Spear" and "The Package," players can destroy T-38 Tyrants by repeatedly bombarding them with heavy firepower from Scorpions and Wraith tanks.

MANUFACTURER: Assembly Forges
DESIGNATION: Type-38 Anti-Aircraft Cannon
AMMUNITION: Ultra-Heavy Plasma Bolts
ENERGY CAPACITY: Unlimited
HEIGHT: 149.5ft (45.6m)
LENGTH: 139.8ft (42.6m)
FIRING MODE: Burst

360-degree rotational range

Firing channel

Fortification platform

The Tyrant's core reactor, its proverbial Achilles' heel, is located within the weapon's fortified base.

PINNACLE OF EVOLUTION

Halo has a history of great large-scale, symmetrical multiplayer maps, but many consider Valhalla to be the pinnacle. This is largely due to the impressive balancing of infantry and vehicle combat.

Some consider Valhalla the spiritual successor to Blood Gulch, but its undulating terrain, slithering river, and discretely compartmentalized areas set it apart from all precursors.

STATISTICS

HALO 3

The Valhalla map easily serves Team Slayer purposes, but team objective gametypes were its forte thanks to its symmetry and division of space.

ENVIRONMENT: Two bases, narrow gorge
RELEVANCE: Ark installation
LAYOUT: Large-scale symmetrical battlefield
PLAYER COUNT: 8 to 16
KEY WEAPONS: Spartan Laser, Sniper Rifle

Valhalla is set on the Ark, with the installation's enormous arm rising into the distant sky.

FORERUNNER CANYON

A verdant rift carved along a Forerunner wall and set within one of the Ark's many mountain ranges, the Halo 3 map Valhalla is easily one of the game's most memorable spaces. Composed of two looming structures on either side of a winding gorge, Valhalla plays into Halo 3's incredible vehicle combat by compartmentalizing the battlefield into distinct locations while still maintaining long lines of sight and freedom of movement.

199

VAMPIRE
TYPE-29 CLOSE-SUPPORT FIGHTER

The Vampire provided close air support and air interdiction solutions for groundside troops in the early years of the Covenant War, especially in engagements involving a heavy concentration of enemy aircraft.

STATISTICS

HALO WARS

In Halo Wars, the Vampire's unique "Stasis Drain" can be highly effective.

MANUFACTURER: Assembly Forges
DESIGNATION: Type-29 Close Support Fighter
CREW: 1 pilot
LENGTH: 49.6ft (15.1m)
WIDTH: 46.4ft (14.1m)
PRIMARY ARMAMENT: Heavy Needle Cannon
SECONDARY ARMAMENT: Medium Plasma Cannon (2)
TERTIARY ARMAMENT: Stasis Cannon

AUTOMATED FIREPOWER

The Vampire's twin flanking plasma cannons automatically track and fire on enemy targets by way of an actuator plug, which is intermittently controlled by the vehicle's pilot.

Cockpit

Heavy Needle Cannon

The Vampire's stasis weapon is quite adaptable, offering an assortment of upgraded variations at the operator's discretion.

Stasis Cannon

Side-mounted Plasma Cannons

ADAPTIVE FIGHTER

The Vampire's main weapon is an augmented variation of Covenant "needle" crystalline technology, though it is also flanked on both sides by mid-grade plasma cannons. In addition to this already impressive arsenal, the T-29 carries a stasis cannon that renders targeted machines immobile and their weapons inert. While the Vampire served the Covenant well for many years, its role was eclipsed by other vehicles with heavier weaponry and higher versatility, as operations tipped from evenly matched combat to cleanup and genocide.

STATISTICS

HALO 3

Players roll through Voi during the Halo 3 mission "The Storm," where they fight through enemy blockades before dealing with the Covenant's anti-aircraft cannon.

PLANET: Earth
COUNTRY: Republic of Kenya, East African Protectorate
GOVERNMENT SITES: Voi Municipal Water Facilities, New Mombasa Waste Management, Voi Greater Outlands Police Bureau
COMMERCIAL SITES: Traxus Heavy Industries, GWC Trans-African Facilities

The town of Voi is a relatively small industrial community located northwest of New Mombasa on Earth. It produces utilities such as power, water, and transportation that support the island megacity.

GHOST TOWN

The small, industry-driven town of Voi was largely uneventful in its mundane service to New Mombasa. On October 20, 2552, a Covenant support fleet began unearthing a massive Forerunner artifact between the town of Voi and New Mombasa, and on November 17, the ancient machine—a Forerunner Portal—was activated. The UNSC and the Covenant battled for control of the site, but the Covenant fled through the Portal to a distant Forerunner installation.

After the Covenant fleet disappeared into the Portal, a Flood-infested ship arrived, initiating the first known Flood outbreak on Earth.

Traxus Factory Complex 09

VULTURE
AC-220 VULTURE GUNSHIP

First made popular during the early years of the rebellion, the AC-220 Vulture gunship is the preferred aerial combat vehicle of the UNSC for protracted air-to-ground engagements.

WITHOUT MERCY

The use of the Vulture against the Insurrection was often viewed as unethical due to the vehicle's obliterative power.

STATISTICS

HALO WARS

Vultures take longer to position than other airborne vehicles, but once they arrive they cannot be ignored.

MANUFACTURER: Ushuaia Armory
DESIGNATION: AC-220 Vulture Gunship
CREW: 2 pilots + 4 crew
LENGTH: 115.1ft (35.1m)
WIDTH: 69.5ft (21.2m)
PRIMARY ARMAMENT: GUA-23/AW/Linkless Feed Autocannons
SECONDARY ARMAMENT: A-74 Sylver Vertical Missile Launcher
TERTIARY ARMAMENT: Argent V Missile Launcher (2)

A-74 Sylver VML

Argent V Launcher

GUA-23/AW Autocannons

The current design for the Vulture was originally conceived in 2498, during the early years of the Insurrection.

DOMINANT GUNSHIP

Deployed against heavily fortified enemy strongholds, the Vulture was originally designed by Reach's Ushuaia Armory to assist the UNSC during the darkest years of the Insurrection. With a pair of GUA-23/AW/ Linkless Feed Autocannons, a twin A-74 Sylver VML, and two Argent V Missile Launchers, a handful of Vultures are easily capable of leveling an enemy stronghold or an entire city. They went on to become irreplaceable in the war against the Covenant.

STATISTICS

HALO: COMBAT EVOLVED
HALO 2 • HALO 3 • HALO WARS
HALO 3: ODST • HALO: REACH

The standard Warthog M41 LAAG can fire in a 360-degree arc thanks to its hydraulic-powered swivel mount.

MANUFACTURER: AMG Transport Dynamics
DESIGNATION: M12 Force Application Vehicle
CREW: 1 driver + 1 gunner + 1 passenger
LENGTH: 19.7ft (6m)
WIDTH: 9.9ft (3m)
PRIMARY ARMAMENT:
M41 Vulcan Light Anti-Aircraft Gun

The standard Warthog is versatile in terms of maneuverability as well as offensive functionality. It operates just as well in a scouting and reconnaissance role as it does applying direct fire.

TRADITIONAL RECON VEHICLE

The Warthog weighs roughly three metric tonnes, is fueled by a 12.0 liter liquid-cooled hydrogen-injected engine, and can reach speeds of up to 78mph (125kph). It is armed by a number of rear-bed turret configurations of varying firepower, ultimately creating a very robust fleet of vehicles. Its widespread use means that every UNSC soldier is familiar with its operation, and that repair and refitting are easy due to the availability of spare parts and its uniform design.

The Warthog features a Graf/Hauptman solar/saline actuator, which can convert 12 liters of fresh, brackish, or salt water into hydrogen.

M41 LAAG

Hydraulic winch system

M41 VULCAN

The M41 is an effective suppression weapon, as it fires about five hundred 12.7 x 99mm rounds per minute.

The M8 Automated Defense System (ADS), known as Wolf Spider, is a networked array of mounted turrets which protect a specific site. The pod-turrets can target, track, and fire on enemy ground and air forces.

STATISTICS

HALO: REACH

When damaged, Wolf Spiders must be manually reset using the keypad, as witnessed in Halo: Reach's "The Package."

MANUFACTURER: Misriah Armory
SERIES: M8 Automated Defense System
AMMUNITION: 12.7 x 99mm
DRUM CAPACITY: 10,000 rounds
HEIGHT: 12.1ft (3.7m)
LENGTH: 13.1ft (4m)
FIRING MODE: Automatic

The M8 ADS is not widely deployed and is exclusively used for sites deemed critical by the Office of Naval Intelligence.

Keypad

Barrel

Optics sensor

TURRET NETWORK

As part of the M8 ADS, Wolf Spiders must be activated individually by way of a keypad. Once they are brought online, they emerge from the pod via a mechanical arm, quickly forming a firing perimeter. The collective turrets operate synchronously as a single machine, sighting and tracking targets, and coordinating overlapping fields of fire to bring down anything entering its area of operation. Targeting is handled via a series of low-mounted optics right below the weapon, dictating a target's vector and distance relative to the gun itself. After sustaining serious damage, the Wolf Spider trips a killswitch, dropping the weapon back into the pod and closing the hatch for protection.

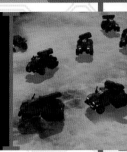

STATISTICS

HALO WARS

The Wolverine appears in Halo Wars and is best against airborne threats.

MANUFACTURER: Ushuaia Armory
DESIGNATION: M9 Main Anti-Air Tank
CREW: 1 driver + 2 gunners
LENGTH: 25.9ft (7.9m)
WIDTH: 14.5ft (4.4m)
PRIMARY ARMAMENT:
M260 Multiple Launch Rocket System
SECONDARY ARMAMENT:
XM511 Heavy Grenade Launcher

MILITARY CAMPAIGNS

Also known as the MAAT-9, the Wolverine was prominently used in military campaigns on Harvest, Arcadia, Dwarka, Miridem, Troy, and Jericho VII.

Over the years, the M9 Main Anti-Aircraft Tank has consistently proven itself in situations requiring the joint application of mobility and anti-air firepower, while still being effective against ground targets.

M260 MLRS

The M9 Wolverine, like the Rocket Warthog, is armed with an MLRS (Multiple Launch Rocket System).

Operator cabin

Half track

UNORTHODOX DESIGN

The M9 Wolverine is somewhat of an enigma within the UNSC in that it is does not have the traditional design or functionality of a conventional tank. Despite its unorthodox half-track configuration, the Wolverine's armament is unquestionably powerful. Its M260 MLRS can swiftly carve airborne targets out of the sky, while its XM511 Heavy Grenade Launcher nullifies encroaching infantry and light armor on the ground.

WRAITH
TYPE-26 ASSAULT GUN CARRIAGE

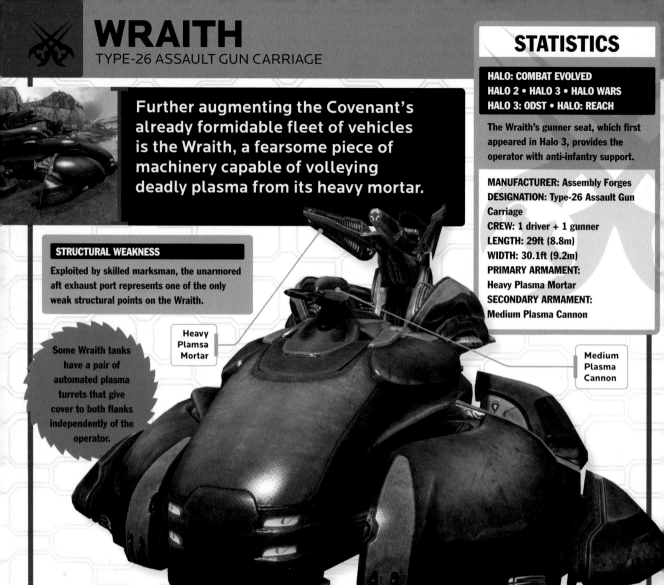

Further augmenting the Covenant's already formidable fleet of vehicles is the Wraith, a fearsome piece of machinery capable of volleying deadly plasma from its heavy mortar.

STATISTICS

HALO: COMBAT EVOLVED
HALO 2 • HALO 3 • HALO WARS
HALO 3: ODST • HALO: REACH

The Wraith's gunner seat, which first appeared in Halo 3, provides the operator with anti-infantry support.

MANUFACTURER: Assembly Forges
DESIGNATION: Type-26 Assault Gun Carriage
CREW: 1 driver + 1 gunner
LENGTH: 29ft (8.8m)
WIDTH: 30.1ft (9.2m)
PRIMARY ARMAMENT: Heavy Plasma Mortar
SECONDARY ARMAMENT: Medium Plasma Cannon

STRUCTURAL WEAKNESS

Exploited by skilled marksman, the unarmored aft exhaust port represents one of the only weak structural points on the Wraith.

Some Wraith tanks have a pair of automated plasma turrets that give cover to both flanks independently of the operator.

Heavy Plamsa Mortar

Medium Plasma Cannon

COVENANT TANK

The Wraith is easily the most prominent heavy armor vehicle the Covenant employ groundside. Its speed and maneuverability rely on a boosted gravity propulsion drive which can deftly toss its 47 ton chassis around the battlefield, while its well-armored frame can easily crush nearby infantry. The real threat of the Wraith is its heavy plasma mortar, which hurls super-heated plasma projectiles capable of eliminating fortified and dug-in enemies. This already formidable armament is also bolstered by a medium plasma cannon manned by a separate gunner.

STATISTICS

HALO 2 • HALO 3

Zanzibar excels at objective-based gametypes, specifically those centered on round-based, offensive and defensive combat.

ENVIRONMENT: Base, beach, walls
RELEVANCE: EAP Wind Power Station
LAYOUT: Asymmetrical, objective-based
PLAYER COUNT: 8 to 16
KEY WEAPONS: Sniper Rifle, Rocket Launcher (Halo 2), Spartan Laser (Halo 3)

Zanzibar was one of Halo's first objective-focused multiplayer maps. It was here that players learned to stay on their toes every round and adjust their play style to meet the demands of both offense and defense.

BEACH AND BASE

Offense begins on the beautiful, ruin-strewn Zanzibar beach and defense in the dark interior of an abandoned wind power station. The battlefield between them is varied and diverse: an enormous sea wall, a massive power-generating turbine fan, a number of elevated perches, and plenty of room for vehicles. Halo 2's Zanzibar and Halo 3's Last Resort both showed just how addictive team-based objective gametypes could be. Many maps have since featured this rather basic concept of offense and defense, but few could argue that any have pulled it off as elegantly and as successfully as Zanzibar.

Zanzibar and Last Resort take place at Wind Power Station 7, on an island off the eastern coast of Africa.

207

LONDON, NEW YORK, MELBOURNE,
MUNICH, AND DELHI

EDITORIAL ASSISTANT: Emma Grange
EDITOR: Lisa Stock
SENIOR EDITOR: Elizabeth Dowsett
DESIGNER: Owen Bennett
MANAGING ART EDITOR: Ron Stobbart
PUBLISHING MANAGER: Catherine Saunders
ART DIRECTOR: Lisa Lanzarini
PUBLISHER: Simon Beecroft
PUBLISHING DIRECTOR: Alex Allan
PRODUCTION EDITOR: Sean Daly
PRODUCTION CONTROLLER: Nick Seston

WRITTEN BY Jeremy Patenaude

ACKNOWLEDGMENTS
Dorling Kindersley would like to thank
Rick Achberger, Laura Akers, Jacob Benton,
Christine Finch, Kevin Grace, Tyler Jeffers,
Frank O'Connor, Corrinne Robinson, and
Charles Webb with 343 Industries at Microsoft.

343 Industries would like to thank
Bungie Studios, Scott Dell'Osso, Nick
Dimitrov, David Figatner, Josh Kerwin, Bryan
Koski, Matt McCloskey, Paul Patinios, Bonnie
Ross-Ziegler, Phil Spencer, and Carla Woo.
343 Industries would also like to thank
Stephen Loftus, who provided his expertise
and insight into the Halo Universe for the
betterment of this book.

And thanks also to every Halo fan for keeping
the fight against the Covenant going for ten
awesome years.

First published in the United States in 2011
by DK Publishing
375 Hudson Street
New York, New York 10014

11 12 13 14 15 10 9 8 7 6 5 4 3 2 1
179626—05/11

Color reproduction by Media Development Printing, UK
Printed and bound in the United States by Lake Book Manufacturing, Inc.

Discover more at
www.dk.com